A Fireside Book
Published by Simon & Schuster

New York  London  Toronto  Sydney  Tokyo  Singapore

# LOST LOVERS, FOUND FRIENDS

## Maintaining Friendship
## after the Breakup

▼

# SCOTT NELSON, Ph.D.

**FIRESIDE**
Simon & Schuster Building
Rockefeller Center
1230 Avenue of the Americas
New York, New York 10020

Designed by Diane Stevenson/SNAP·HAUS GRAPHICS

Manufactured in the United States of America

1  3  5  7  9  10  8  6  4  2

Library of Congress Cataloging in Publication Data
Nelson, Scott.
Lost lovers, found friends: maintaining friendship after the breakup/
Scott Nelson.
p.  cm.
"A Fireside book."
Includes bibliographical references and index.
1. Divorced people—United States—Psychology.  2. Separation
(Psychology)  3. Friendship—United States.  4. Interpersonal
relations.  I. Title.
HQ834.N45  1991
306.89—dc20                                               91-2973
CIP
ISBN 0-671-70109-6

# Acknowledgments

On the long journey to bring this book to fruition, I have received extraordinary encouragement, support, and assistance from many people.

To my partner, Jeri Marlowe, I extend my greatest appreciation and love. Her love, patience, and passion have often made it possible for me to go the distance. Particularly in the final, harried days prior to submitting the completed manuscript, her abiding affirmations and tenderness were just what the doctor ordered. The importance of the hours she gave in editing of the original proposal and the final draft of the book was enormous. The intellectual challenges she offered to the emerging content often breathed refreshing life into the work.

Lonnie Barbach left me agape when she returned the first full draft to me ornate with comments and suggestions which I am certain made the final version exceedingly more accessible. Her generosity, encouragement, and friendship are priceless.

There were many people at the MRI in Palo Alto who, from the first time that I presented the idea for this book, have been important sources of moral support. Arthur Bodin, Ph.D., Victoria Wendling, Benjamin Hammett, Ph.D., Joyce Emamjomeh, and Sharon Wear all showed remarkable patience and kindness throughout the project.

Thanks also to Jim Purcell who, with his typical gentle sincerity, sparked the original idea for the book.

Faith Childs, my agent, had the vision necessary to move the book from proposal to reality. She has been remarkably available and helpful every step of the way. Her gentle, respectful, but clearly professional posture has been much appreciated.

From my first contact with my editor, Malaika Adero, at Simon & Schuster, I appreciated her warm, yet professional style. When I received her editorial comments and suggestions on the first draft I was pleasantly astounded by her obvious skill with the written word. I learned much from her suggestions and feel certain that the readability of the final product is markedly enhanced by her contribution. Also, I must thank Ellen Garvey for her skillful line editing of the last draft of the book. Again, what I learned from reading her suggested revisions was truly an education in itself.

Many thanks to Michael Marlowe for reading drafts of the manuscript and for his very thoughtful suggestions.

The individuals who participated in the lengthy interviews were of course indispensable. I am forever grateful for their willingness to share their experiences and insights, some of which were obviously painful.

My sons, Peter and James Nelson, deserve much credit for the inspirational role that they play in my life. There have been many times when, pressed by book deadlines, I have been unavailable to support them, yet they pressed on to make me proud. In stressful moments their loving injunctions to "chill out" have often brought me back to my senses. Thanks guys!!

# Dedication

I dedicate this book to my parents, Lois and Scott Nelson. As the publication of this book was being negotiated, my father died. Kicked in the stomach by this loss, I could hardly breathe. He was not only my father, he was a dear friend. We had differences, yet we had love and a desire to transcend our differences.

I remember a walk we had in the snow some years ago. My father/friend confessed that despite his life of love and his love of life, he was disappointed that he could not confront certain changes in attitude within himself with an open heart. I believe that in his painful confession was also a challenge: a challenge to open my heart and mind to the possibilities and not the limitations of our existence. I extend this challenge to you—this opportunity to open your heart and mind for your benefit.

I was buoyed by the gracious efforts of my mother who seemed to so valiantly overcome the loss of her husband. Unlike myself, she doesn't talk much. Nevertheless, I was spurred on by her willingness to work toward the future and take her life, with passion, into her own hands. It is to these two people—the inspiration of their love while together, and their courage while apart—that I dedicate this book.

# Contents

▼

# Contents

▼

# Introduction

At a recent wedding I leaned over to the fellow sitting next to me and asked, "How is it that you come to this wedding?"

"Well, the bride and I were involved some years ago. After we broke up as lovers, we just became good friends," he said with a glimmer in his eye. Looking around the room it occurred to me that at least twenty people at the gathering had previously been couples. Some had been married and some had committed themselves to each other without formal marriage; now they are all uncoupled, but still good friends. Each had accrued a range of benefits from their continued, albeit altered, intimate connection.

Much has been written about *individual* survival and growth following breakup or divorce; in stark contrast, little information about *postbreakup relationships* has been published either in scientific or popular literature. Even less information is available about *friendly* relationships after uncoupling. This yawning gap seems due, in part, to three widespread but erroneous assumptions:

1. that friendly relationships after breakup simply do not exist
2. that divorce or breakup *should* be the end of a relationship and if the relationship continues it must be based upon pathological connection between the ex-partners
3. there is no real benefit for ex-partners in remaining friends but only more pain.

During the process of interviewing people for this book, I was repeatedly struck by how many people actually rejected these long-held assumptions, yet reported receiving intense pressure from their friends, family, and even colleagues and counselors to not maintain friendships with their ex-partners. They said that most of their friends accused them of being "crazy" for remaining in contact with their ex-partners. To many lay and professional people alike, the idea that a truly meaningful and beneficial friendship can emerge out of the ashes of an intimate love relationship is ill-considered and supremely idealistic. "How can you possibly feel all of the pain that you feel and even consider becoming friends with your ex-partner?" they ask.

Jackie, a thirty-five-year-old lawyer, put it in a nutshell:

*I often feel guilty and confused for trying to be friends with David [her ex-husband]. When I talk about our efforts to be friends despite the divorce, other friends and even the counselors in the divorce workshops always tell me I'm a fool or "not confronting the true reality." We have children together so it's important that we at least maintain a working relationship. But even if we didn't have children I know that he has always meant a lot to me. I don't want to lose all that I get from him. Your research just by its existence gives me courage.*

A recent exchange in a Miss Manners column reveals a bit about the current public attitude and concern over the continuing role of ex-partners in our lives.

*Dear Miss Manners:*

*I have just received a wedding invitation from my ex-daughter-in-law. I have always loved her dearly, and she is the mother of three of my granddaughters. It will be a small wedding. Would it be in good taste for me to attend?*

*Gentle Reader:*

*Let's see whose taste this might offend. Not that of your former daughter-in-law or her families old and new—otherwise she wouldn't have invited you. Not that of Miss Manners, who commends maintaining good family relations after divorce, only drawing the line at a former spouse's attending a wedding to a successor, as the irony is far too interesting a treat for the guests.*

*That leaves your son and perhaps a current daughter-in-law. Miss*

*Manners urges you to consider whether this would be highly objectionable
to them.*[1]

While it appears that Miss Manners is heading in the right
direction, she falls short in the end and joins the ranks of those
who would place arbitrary limits on what is truly possible.
Moreover, a 1978 survey of therapists, lawyers, and clergy
revealed that a full 85 percent of these professionals said that
they would *not* recommend that their clients attempt to maintain
a friendship with their ex-partners.[2] In my experience, little has
changed in the intervening years.

Despite this stereotypical skepticism, many people *have* made
the transition from lovers to friends. A 1988 dissertation study
of postdivorce relationships by Carol Masheter revealed that
nearly 50 percent of the people interviewed reported "friendly"
feelings for their ex-spouses and that at least 25 percent of the
total group had contact at least once a week. Some ex-spouses *do*
maintain friendly contact after divorce. It is also important to
remember that the millions of legally married couples that divorce
each year represent only a portion of the couples in intimate
relationships who break up each year. Unfortunately, statistics on
unmarried cohabiting couples who uncouple are nearly impossible to obtain. We could certainly learn a great deal about the
dynamics of successful relationships from this uncounted, unin-
vestigated group struggling with similar breakup and transition
issues.

The assumption that divorce or unmarried breakups *should*
end up with complete separation and lack of contact is founded
on the heretofore inadequately examined belief that remaining
"friends" only reveals that the individuals have not faced the fact
of the loss of the couple relationship. It may appear that they are

dependently clinging to the old relationship. Recent research findings reported in Carol Masheter's dissertation and in the Constance Ahrons and Roy Rodgers book *Divorced Families: Meeting the Challenge of Divorce and Remarriage*, along with my work clearly indicates that for at least some portion of the people who break up, a "healthy" postdivorce relationship can be achieved.[3] According to Masheter,

> *The findings indicated that a considerable number of divorced persons have ongoing relationships with their exspouses which are not necessarily characterized by unhealthy dependence and disruptive quarreling and in some cases may promote postdivorce parenting or meet legitimate adult needs for extended family and friendship.*

Healthy "friendly" contact with ex-lovers and ex-spouses is possible after the breakup, and there are many legitimate *benefits* to be gained from working through the transition from lovers to friends. My intention is to show you how the transition can be made and what reward you may find in continuing and cultivating friendship with someone who is no longer your partner.

*Lost Lovers, Found Friends* is the first book which makes the case for and focuses upon the *successful* transition from an intimate couple relationship to friendship after a breakup or divorce. My conclusions are based on twenty years of clinical experience and seventy-five in-depth interviews with clients, friends, and associates. I will give you new information not only about the dynamics of individual postbreakup relationships but about the emerging social phenomenon of remaining friends after uncoupling as well.

# The Task at Hand

At the point of breaking up you face the specter of unplanned change in your life along with an array of potent feelings that well up from within. These might include fear, anxiety, anger, excitement, depression, wonder, and confusion. The change perhaps most difficult to face is within your most intimate relationship—even if you wanted the change. The uncoupling of a marriage or a relationship involving commitment certainly must rank among the most devastating of all relationship changes. For all involved, "breaking up is (definitely) hard to do."

One approach to coping with the nauseating whirlwind of conflicting feelings that accompany divorce or separation is to simply escape—to run away and try to forget. There are many methods for running away, of course. By refusing to communicate, using anger assaultively, or actually leaving the area, we physically or emotionally distance ourselves. Or we may slump into depression, abuse drugs, or flee into excessive work.

A more positive way that some people attempt to handle the changes that come with divorce or separation is by courageously struggling with the pain of losing the relationship and turning their eyes solely toward their own personal growth. They leave the relationship behind as they seek to create a new feeling about themselves and a new direction for their lives. This approach is the thrust of most current growth-oriented approaches to surviving separation and divorce.

There are, no doubt, situations in which escape from and even complete abandonment of a once-important relationship is the healthy thing to do. For example, it may be wise to end an abusive relationship with nothing left to salvage for a worthwhile friendship. Sometimes you just have to cut your losses and move on. We'll talk about the issues involved in making this decision later in this book.

While there may be good reasons for abandoning the relationship altogether, the guiding premise of this book is that in many situations such an extreme decision is unnecessary. It's like throwing the baby out with the bath water. The experiences of those interviewed serve as living testimony for this premise. Indeed, as you will see, the *benefits* of struggling to clean up the relationship between two people who have previously been a couple can be great and enriching for both.

## The Source of the Information

In my clinical practice over the past twenty years I have often worked with couples who come to me initially saying that they want to work on their marriage or relationship. But many of these couples were really seeking some way to dissolve the marriage without risking the total loss from their lives of a person they loved. In part, *Lost Lovers, Found Friends* is based upon many hours of our tripartite struggles to find a way.

The information in this book is also based upon detailed interviews with seventy-five individuals from many parts of the country. The participants were not selected using strict random sampling methods but rather were recruited via newspaper and bulletin board advertisements, personal contacts, and referrals from other participants. They do not represent the complete range of differences among people living in the United States. I did, nonetheless, attempt to select as diverse a group as possible, representing multiple races, age groups, ethnic and religious backgrounds, and types of coupled relationships.

I selected primarily those individuals and couples who perceived themselves as having successfully made the transition from lovers to healthy friends because I suspected that they know what many others do not. While I recognize that there might be *some* advantage to knowing whether they are really healthy, there remains tremendous controversy in the professional and lay community as to just exactly what we mean by *healthy* in the first place. Further, life and relationships are *processes.* Many of the couples I interviewed did not become friends immediately after the breakup, and I suspect many of you who are not friends with your ex-partner today may find that you will be at some future time.

As relationships go through dramatic changes, including breakup, personal accounts of past relationships often reflect only one perspective on the current friendship. Where it was possible I interviewed both members of the previously existing partnership, as I would do to get a better idea of the whole picture in most couples therapy situations. Attention to the similarities or differences of each partner's account of the transition from lover to friend is of some importance, as is each partner's individual perception of what happened and the nature of the relationship today. For example, Clarinda and Joe had separated nine months before I interviewed them. According to Joe, the current relationship was very exciting but tightly controlled and limited. He appreciated that they could work cooperatively and with great success on joint business projects begun while they were a couple. He also very much liked the freedom to call Clarinda on the phone to brainstorm his newest ideas. Joe said that he still needed distance, and that this arrangement was necessary for the security of the new relationship in which he was involved.

Clarinda was basically happy with the friendship but believed it to be much broader in scope. "We're buddies. I can call him any time. It sometimes helps to talk about personal stuff."

Despite the fact that the composite, or objective, view of the relationship indicates clear differences in their definition of the friendship, both nonetheless are obviously pleased.

It comes as no surprise that much of the literature, as well as my clinical experience, suggests that men enter, reside in, and leave relationships differently from women. With this in mind I have taken care to interview both men and women in approximately equal numbers.

Much to my delight, most of the individuals I interviewed said that the questions which made up the interview protocol were, in themselves, helpful. In many cases they spontaneously reported that the questions helped them to clarify the nature of their relationship and helped them to free themselves from certain troubling issues that had been a cause for concern. One couple volunteered that their relationship was much easier after they had individually participated in the interview. As the woman of this couple put it, "There were feelings of loss left over of which neither of us had been aware. When we talked about them after the interview we were both clearer about our friendship and much more at ease."

Another woman, Tanya, said, "When Leo and I talked about our relationship after the interview we became clearer about what we each wanted."

## Some Words of Caution

The emphasis in this book upon the *relationship* after breakup is not intended to imply that *individual* growth and survival in the beginning phases of the breakup process is unimportant. In fact much of this individual work is the foundation for successful transition to friendship with your ex. With this in mind you are encouraged to make the effort to explore the resources listed in the back of the book which will help you with the individual work you may need to accomplish immediately after your breakup.

A woman I interviewed at the beginning of this project pointed out, "you have to be careful when reading all of this psychology stuff. Sometimes it can make you do things that are really not *you.*" Consequently, a skeptical stance in reading this book can be a healthy one. The purpose of this book is to help you think about what *you* want to do with *your* life and, in particular, *your* relationship. As you will discover there are many aspects of the breakup process which most people share. At the same time each person travels a unique path. So while you read the following pages, remember that what is good for you can only be *decided* by *you.* Keep in mind, however, that time changes everything: what is good for you today may change tomorrow.

## Organization of the Book

Each chapter begins with a series of questions for you to consider about your own relationship. I encourage you to write down your own responses to these questions in the space provided at the back of the book. This exercise will be useful for you in two ways. First, you will benefit from organizing your thoughts about your breakup experience. You will better understand the issues with which you are struggling and the future to which you aspire. Secondly, you will benefit from knowing how you have changed over time as you look back at what you were going through this period.

Chapter one confronts the common question, "If they can be friends why did they break up?" It considers the reasons that people decide to end their intimate relationships. It will show you ways to determine whether or not your own relationship is viable.

Chapter two describes the variety of relationships the people I interviewed have successfully worked out for themselves. The intent of the chapter is to reveal the extraordinarily wide range of possibilities available to you as you attempt to forge your own changing relationship.

The many *benefits* of remaining friends are detailed in chapter three. Like the very nature of the relationships themselves, the benefits experienced by the individuals and ex-couples are complex and to some extent unique to each relationship.

Because chapter four focuses upon situations in which continued contact or friendship is *not* recommended after the breakup it may seem like a thematic contradiction or even inappropriate for this book. Nevertheless, there *are* conditions under which friendship is not a good idea or even really possible. In some cases the transition to friendship may be just a matter of timing; in others, no amount of time or change will make the difference. While this may seem like a wet blanket on a barely kindled fire, examining whether friendship is possible is, as I will explain, an important preliminary to exploring how to be friends.

To my knowledge, despite the widespread assumptions held by professionals, about the inappropriateness of friendship after breakup, this chapter is the first serious look at some of the issues involved.

Though the major focus of *Lost Lovers, Found Friends* is on the positive friendship of ex-lovers, you will need to confront your individual growth and development at the transition because of their impact on your potential for continuing your relationship as a friendship. Chapter five, "Taking Care of Yourself," addresses the tasks you must accomplish *individually* to improve the likelihood of a successful transition to friendship.

Chapter six offers specific ways in which ex-partners can help each other make a transition from being lovers to friendship possible. Some of these ideas are abstract or about attitude, while others are more concrete suggestions of actions that I and the participants of the study have found to be helpful.

At the end of the book you will find an annotated bibliography of books on the breakup experience for the individual; you may find these a useful adjunct to this book.

CHAPTER

# 1

## WHOA!! IF THEY CAN BE FRIENDS, WHY DID THESE PEOPLE BREAK UP IN THE FIRST PLACE?

▼

When I've discussed the topic of this book, one of the questions I've heard most frequently has been, "If a couple could be friends, why did they break up in the first place?" Despite the fact that there are millions of people who have, with great benefit, made the transition from lovers to friends, the question is worth addressing. It's important to consider why people break up, why you and your partner decided to break up, because it can lead you to a better understanding of how you can be successful in maintaining a positive connection after you've uncoupled. Also, many of you who question whether you want to leave your current relationship may find it helpful to know why others have disengaged. This is particularly true for those of you who are in relationships that, at least on the surface seem like satisfactory unions.

The reasons why couples break up can be reduced to three categories: first, individual problems within one (or both) members of the couple, such as difficulty with intimacy or in making a commitment; second, critical differences in attitude, life-style, and beliefs between the individual partners; and third, external factors such as changes in job status, health, or living conditions.

As you will discover, none of these categories of reasons *necessarily* rules out continued friendship between those who ended their relationship as lovers.

**Individual (Intrapersonal) Issues.** Individual, intrapersonal issues are those that we cope with alone. They are problems that exist independent of our romantic partners. They may be related to past experiences or even present experiences that are not shared with our lover and can cause feelings of depression, low self-esteem, anger, lack of energy, or chronic health problems. One clue that the problem that has led to your desire to break up is individual in nature is, of course, that you have experienced the problem in other romantic relationships.

In Joan's case, when her father died, she decided that she had to break up with John in order to have the time and emotional energy to cope with this sudden tragedy. She said that her difficulty in staying in the relationship was not due to John or problems in the marriage but rather to her commitment to her family and her own overwhelming sense of disorientation and depression that accompanied her father's death.

*I think that it was important for me that the problem between us was not intimacy but rather commitment. My personal situation in which our relationship occurred made it impossible for me to commit to him. Because my father had died I felt that I had to be with my family. It was as though John really didn't exist. I had to go to my family and to take care of myself.*

It could be argued that if Joan and John had a truly committed relationship in the first place she would have perceived him as a resource rather than a burden. True, but the fact was that he wasn't a resource from *her* perspective *at the time.* Joan clearly had much unfinished business in relation to her father and her family of origin that superseded her need to make a commitment to John.

Daphne Rose Kingma in her book, *Coming Apart: Why Relationships End and How to Live Through the Ending of Yours* points out that people often come together in a relationship because interaction with the partner provides an opportunity to work through a developmental task. Some of these developmental tasks are tasks that were left incomplete while growing up in the original birth family. For example, a basic task of human development is to learn to be able to trust others. Some individuals have not accomplished this basic sense of trust and try to acquire it through their adult relationships. Other developmental tasks are related to what are considered normal stages or processes of human social and psychological development in the life of an adult, like giving birth, creating a family, contributing to the community as an adult, or working.

If you have incomplete developmental tasks, your partner, who behaves in many ways like your parent or sibling, may offer, merely by his or her presence, an opportunity to work through issues left incomplete with your real parent. Once this developmental task is complete, if a new kind of relationship is not successfully negotiated, you may want to move on from the relationship. This source of breakup might be more correctly considered both an individual and couple difference.

Raised in a dysfunctional family that included nine siblings, Beth, a sixty-year-old beautician, had little opportunity to express herself as an individual. Her father, a cruel alcoholic, had been both controlling of those around him and out of control himself. Her situation is a good example of a breakup which was precipitated by one partner's need to move forward on developmental issues related to family of origin.

Beth explained that through most of her childhood, she was

rarely able to know when she was doing things correctly and when she was not. Growing up in this family, Beth did not believe that she had any life as an individual. Also, she was required to avoid asserting herself in any way as an individual. In her struggle to survive this very difficult situation, Beth needed to *dissociate* her feelings, that is, cut her feelings away from her consciousness. At the age of fifteen, Beth married a man from a foreign country who promised to take her away to a new life. Unfortunately, as Beth soon found out, her new husband and his family were also very controlling, and offered her little opportunity to express herself as a person. While she was not conscious of it for the thirty years of her marriage, Beth struggled to try to complete two important developmental tasks which were related to the traumatic experiences in her family of origin. First, she wanted to gain some control over her life by beginning to make decisions that would lead her in a direction that would be fulfilling *for herself*. Second, and perhaps as an extension of her first task, she needed to learn how to express herself as an individual so that revealing who she was to the world would not result in a devastatingly frightening experience.

Beth's leap forward, which was the beginning of the end of her marriage, came as an unexpected result of a vacation offered to her by a friend. Assuming that she and her friends would be spending their time together, Beth was not at all concerned about going on vacation without her husband. Her husband, accustomed to being the lord of the house, reluctantly "allowed" her to go. To her surprise, when she and her friends reached their destination, Beth was given a key to the condo and told, "have a good time!" She was left completely on her own for perhaps the first time in her life. After an initial period of near panic, she spent five days reading, walking on the beach, and basically coming to know herself as an individual without the pressure of her husband, children, or other people telling her who she should be.

When she returned home, very conscious of the developmental tasks that she needed to accomplish, she tried to explain her situation to her husband. When he refused to understand or to support her growth, and in fact threatened to have her locked up in an asylum for the insane, she realized, "I had to make a decision to live or to die. I could not go back to the way that I was." She had to leave the relationship to continue to grow.

Today, it's very hard to imagine Beth as that frightened, nonassertive, invisible person she described herself to be some twelve years ago. Now she recognizes herself as an intelligent, articulate, much individuated person, clear that her divorce from her ex-husband was an essential step in her movement toward self-actualization. By the age of forty-eight she finally accomplished a personal developmental task which less oppressed individuals accomplish by the time they are young adults.

In contrast to Beth's experience, Megan decided that she needed to break up with her partner, Ray, because at the age of thirty-five she felt that it was time for her to have a child and settle into a more stable family life-style. This developmental task of childbearing and initiating a family was not breaking the chains of her past as in Beth's situation but rather fulfilling an archetypal dream. While having a child in the physical sense may not be an essential part of normal human development, bringing *something* into the world seems to be an important part of the adult life experience of most people. Unfortunately Ray already had two children and was hoping for more time to develop himself as an individual after already having given much of his time to his children over the past several years. It was probably helpful that Megan and Ray had only been together for six months, in that they were less invested in each other. Nevertheless, as it became clear that Megan needed to find another partner with whom she could move forward on her own developmental path, she and Ray were compelled to spend many hours reassuring each other that their decision to separate was best for both and reaffirming their desire to remain friends.

**Interpersonal Differences.** The differences between partners usually happen as a result of their individual needs, desires, or tastes. Sometimes it is difficult to distinguish whether or not the difficulties which lead to breakups are of an inter- or intrapersonal nature. Generally speaking, when the decision to end the relationship is mutual, the primary issue informing the decision is interpersonal and follows mutual attempts and failures to make the problems go away.

John and Tina's experience is an example of one where intra- and interpersonal issues lead to a breakup. John is a thirty-five-year-old engineering executive who was divorced from his first wife three years ago and who is emotionally very closely connected to his children. When John met Tina, he felt that their relationship could be easily integrated with his relationship with his children. After a time, however, it became clear that trying to meet the needs of his children as well as the needs of his partner caused conflict. John began to feel increasingly guilty, confused, upset, and stressed. Even though he attempted to understand these feelings in therapy, he was still unable to come to a comfortable resolution. He broke off the relationship with Tina because he could not contain his feelings of guilt and discomfort about not taking adequate care of his own children or about feeling split.

Sexual differences are often the cause of strained relationships. Partners disagree over how often sex should take place, in

their attitudes towards sex in general, and in specific sexual be-
haviors, as well as in their sexual history.

As a therapist, I often work with couples in which one partner was sexually abused as a child. In the aftermath of child
sexual abuse, the survivor carries with her or him a constellation
of very conflicted feelings about being sexual. Ironically, these
feelings increase in intensity as the level of intimacy rises in an
adult, intimate, couple relationship. While the following case example may be extreme, a similar tug of war can emerge with just
about any couple, whether sexual abuse is a part of its personal
history or not.

Edgar, an electronics engineer, and June, his wife, have been
married for about ten years. In the glow of newness at the beginning of their relationship, their sexual experience was very positive and satisfying for both of them, but as time moved on the
glow faded and a discrepancy in their individual desires for intimacy emerged. Edgar described a sudden change in the amount
of physical affection and more specifically the types of sexual
activity that they each desired and offered the other. June wanted
much less, if any, contact and Edgar wanted intense sexual activity at least two or three times a week. In addition to their difference in desire there was also a difference in the *meaning* of being
sexual. June had repeatedly been sexually abused as a child by an
older neighbor boy. She began to see being sexually available as a
kind of oppression; she was being forced to do something against
her will by both her internal beliefs and by Edgar. As June began
to withdraw sexually, Edgar felt rejected, angry, and resentful.
They were both uncomfortable communicating about their sexual needs and that, of course, made matters worse. In contrast to
their sexual relationship, much of the rest of their involvement
together was very positive. Nevertheless, after ten years and no
improvement in their situation, Edgar made the decision to an-

swer his need to be validated as a sexual person and to find some way of having his sexual needs met. Despite the other positive aspects of their partnership, after much discussion, they decided to break up. June was very disappointed but agreed that they would have to go their own ways. This vignette demonstrates how the distinction between intrapersonal issues—June's struggles with sexuality, Edgar's struggle with disappointment and rejection—and interpersonal issues can become blurred. Was there something that they as a couple could have done differently? It is hard to tell.

In addition to sexual discrepancies, other differences which sometimes go unnoticed in the early, euphoric stages of a relationship can gradually tear away at partner's commitment to each other. Usually these are differences in life-style or beliefs and attitudes about the way the world, relationships, or life should operate. These attitudes or beliefs can be seen as the values that the individuals have received either from their own unique family culture or from their participation in their subcultures of school, friends, clubs, churches. The reason that these beliefs or attitudes have such great impact upon us is that they help us navigate in a world that really has no absolute reality, no true, right reality. Without a clear, true reality, we must create and then cling to our own in order to feel consistent. Sometimes, our beliefs are different from our partner's on matters of real significance, such as the role of other friends or religion. Often this kind of difference is the "difference that makes the difference" and can lead to the couples' decision to separate.

Greta, a thirty-year-old therapist and Max, a thirty-one-year-old carpenter, decided to break up essentially because of religious differences. Greta and Max got together two and a half years before, while they were living in a religious community in the Midwest. Greta was at times unhappy but in general found ways to cope with her concerns about some disturbing tenets of the religion in which they were involved.

Once they moved to the West so that Max could be closer to the religious leader he revered, Greta said their relationship began to come apart. Max's increased commitment to the organization became a problem in part because of the attitudes that this religion took toward the role of men and women in a marriage and in society. Following the teachings of the leader, Max believed that women had a lesser role to play in the church and in family life and that the couple relationship itself was of lesser value than his relationship to the church. Greta disagreed with each of these attitudes. After much struggle and many long conversations, it became clear to Greta that Max was becoming increasingly involved in the organization and rigid in his belief that a woman's role is one of subservience to men. His behavior became more and more damaging to her self-esteem. In addition to and perhaps related to these differences, Greta began to see differences in the way in which they felt about their relationship independent of the religion. She wanted more time for them to be together, to have a more active sexual life, and to share housekeeping duties. She loved Max's sense of humor, his ability to think clearly about financial matters, and the good parts of the history that they shared together but after seeking the advice of both friends and family members, Greta ultimately decided to leave him.

Similarly, Lynn, a thirty-four-year-old legal secretary said:

*I knew we were drifting apart. When he decided to join the [unnamed] personal development program it felt like there was no way in which we could stay together. He saw it as his chance, I saw it as him being fooled. I still cared about him but couldn't buy into his plan.*

**External Forces.** Events and forces external to the couple relationship can also lead to breakup. Changes in job situations, career opportunities, and the demands of children or aging family members can unfortunately put a wedge between members of a couple. While it is true that some transcontinental marriages survive, the stress of distance may be deadly to the sense of coupleness.

Tim, a thirty-five-year-old mining engineer, and Sarah, a computer programmer working in California, had been married for five years when Tim was offered an extraordinary career opportunity in Colorado. It meant that they would be separate for the first six months. They discussed the issues and mutually decided that it would be best for both of them for Tim to take the opportunity. The engineering job lasted three years; at that point, he was offered another job in an even more remote location. It too was very exciting and promised to deliver to him what was most important and meaningful in his life. Sarah also wanted to be more involved in her career as computer programmer.

After about a year and a half, Sarah and Tim began to feel that their long-distance relationship was becoming increasingly difficult to manage and felt less and less committed to each other. They both had great respect for each other and profoundly understood and appreciated each other's commitment to their respective careers. So, despite their concern for each other they decided to discontinue the marriage and maintain the friendship. They were childless and saw no reason to try to continue the marriage with the geographical difference between them. This stress of distance takes its toll on marital relationships, even those of celebrities, as illustrated by the separation of Barbara Walters and her husband, Merv Adelson. As Liz Smith wrote in a gossip article, "The many friends of the couple on both coasts know that Merv and Barbara are still deeply devoted to one another. It sounds like a cliche, but I believe they will remain the closest of friends." [1]

## Type of Breakup and the Transition Experience

Couples who separate due to external factors seem to make the transition from lovers to friends with the least difficulty. They tend not to blame each other for their problems. Without blame, there is one less formidable obstacle to maintaining friendship.

Where the breakup was forced by problems of one individual, as was the case with Joan, and is recognized as such by both partners, the transition to friendship is also much less difficult. But it is often difficult to determine whether an individual is, let's say, depressed because of the relationship or because of circumstances unrelated to the relationship. Breakups precipitated by individual, emotional problems are sometimes more difficult to sort out and lower the chances for postbreakup friendship.

When differences of attitudes or beliefs are the basis for the breakup, remaining friends is often difficult. Under these circumstances, people have a hard time accepting the validity of their partner's beliefs and calling their own beliefs and attitudes into question. A struggle over who's right and who's wrong often persists which only leads to more distance and less understanding. An ongoing futile power struggle can be the result. It is difficult for people to accept that their beliefs are not absolute truths. When their beliefs are projected onto their partners, the most effective way for those partners to relieve themselves from the anxiety that this causes is to distance themselves. Unfortunately, out of sight, out of mind does not apply here; sooner or later the crisis will emerge again.

Among breakups in which one or both of the members of the couple clearly has difficulty with intimacy and commitment, the separation and the attempt to transition to friends seemed to have been either a particularly difficult time or paradoxically easy. The source of fear of intimacy in a relationship may not be clear-cut. That is, when intimacy is the issue, a reason for difficulty in handling the breakup is that the foundation of intimacy—a sense of basic trust—might be the result of either private, personal conflicts being confronted by one member, or, alternatively, might be an issue within a relationship in which there have been incidents of broken trust. As we all know, trust once broken is most difficult to regain. In this situation it is important that the couple explore the real reason for the breakup with a third party —preferably a therapist of some skill—so that the situation is made clear and each is left with some real understanding of the partner and of problems as a couple.

These categorizations of factors that lead to disengagement are general statements about why some couples break up. To help yourself make decisions about your situation in a troubled relationship try using the simple comparative listing of the conflicts below. These are what many people in my study listed as grounds for breakup. This list is not meant to serve as a description of the "right" reasons but rather simply the common reasons that some couples decided to throw in the towel on their romantic relationship.

**sexual differences**
**financial struggles**
**depression and lack of energy for the relationship**
**career or job changes leading to emotional and geographical distance between the partners**
**philosophical differences**
**persistent negative or miscommunication**
**drugs and alcohol**
**disputes over responsibilities**

**jealousy and possessiveness**
**demanding and critical behavior**
**a constant feeling of being taken for granted**
**conflicting body clocks and schedules, e.g., different sleep**
**patterns or uncoordinated work schedules**
**conflicting needs for companionship**
**conflicting ideas regarding roles, e.g., parenting styles,**
**work habits**
**dislike for partner's friends**
**chronic illness of one member which left the relationship**
**in some way unfulfilling for the other partner**

Again, this list does not represent good or bad reasons for breaking up, but simply reasons given by people interviewed. What is important about this list is that the items are reasons which precipicated the breakup of couples but *did not spoil* their chances for friendship because of the *way* in which they were handled. Each reason for breakups can be handled in ways that result in and insure friendship and positive renegotiation of the relationship.

CHAPTER

# 2

# FRIENDSHIP AFTER THE BREAKUP:
## A yearly phone call, someone I can count on in a pinch, one of my best friends

▼

*As Henry Murray once said about individuals, we can assume that every relationship is like all other relationships, like some other relationships, and like no other relationship.* [1]

## What is *friendship?*

Friendship, at first glance, as an idea and as an experience is so familiar that discussion of its meaning may seem without value. But I encourage you to take the time to grapple with its meaning by considering the following questions:

1. What is your definition of a friend?
2. How are the friendships you have different from each other?
3. Do you have other kinds of relationships with people that are of value to you but which you would not consider "friendships"? What are these relationships like?
4. What could a friend do or say that would make you want to give up on a friendship completely? Are there friendships that you once enjoyed but which have slipped away?

5. What is your relationship with your ex-partner(s) like now?
6. How would you want your relationship with your ex-partner to be different in the future? (What would you do together? How would you speak to each other? How much time would you spend together?)
7. What is stopping you from maintaining or deepening your friendship with your ex-partner?
8. What do you want from friendships and what are you willing to give to a friendship?

Though diverse and personal, "ideal" friendship as described by the people I interviewed for this book includes a connection with another in which there is a measure of trust and caring; a willingness in both friends to share intimate aspects of their lives; a kind of mutuality or give and take; and a mutual acceptance of the other for who they are. For some people to remain friends would require also some enduring shared interests and activities. But while shared activities were important to some, others indicated that a shared history in itself was often enough to sustain a friendship. They gained from friendly *interactions*, but the simple feeling of having a friend regardless of the amount or kind of interaction was vitally important.

These idealized versions of the meaning and importance of friendship are significant because they indicate the dream of friendship to which we might all aspire. But to enact a successful transition from lovers to friends demands a clearer understanding of what your real friendship needs entail. Soon after I began my interviews for this book, I became aware that the ideal definitions of friendship which people gave me at the beginning of the interview were often quite different from the reality of the relationships they described and revealed later on.

To some extent these differences in the way we understand friendship in the ideal world of ideas versus the real world of experience may explain why, despite a widespread skepticism about maintaining friendship after breakup, millions of people have done it successfully. While postbreakup friendships may not live up to the abstract ideal of friendship, neither do friendships in general.

Here are some of the ways in which actual friendships maintained in everyday life were different from the abstract ideal notion of friendship. Please do not interpret this information as an attempt to get you to accept less than you desire for yourself in your important friendships. Rather, reexamining some false limitations imposed by your definition of friendship can open a door to successful creation of *your* friendships.

**Time Together.** Practically every person I interviewed initially said that simply "spending time" together was an important aspect of friendship. But the actual importance of time together was clearly different depending upon the kind of relationship, each person's current social situation, and geographical proximity.

The kind of relationship friends share also affects their impression of the importance of "time together." Both Joe and Clarinda felt that the most important components of their postbreakup friendship were the opportunity to share and test their ideas with each other and to feel accepted by each other. Joe might seek out Clarinda's input on an idea for a new approach to making his business more robust; he trusted her judgment in such matters. Clarinda, having returned from a weekend retreat, found it invaluable to share new elements of her self-discovery. Given these limited goals for the friendship, they both felt satisfied with rather infrequent contact that had a marked spontaneous quality.

What seemed most important for them was the *availability* of the other.

The social situation of the ex-partners also makes a difference in how they feel about the amount of time they spend together. Priscilla offered an example of a changing social situation which altered her feeling about the amount of time she and her ex-husband, George, spend together. Immediately following their breakup, Priscilla felt that "we never had enough time together." Now that she has started a new job and has a new relationship, she has less time for her friendship with George and is less worried about not spending time together. She went on to say, however, that she was surprised that her feeling of affection and support in the friendship with George did not drop off as time spent together decreased. She was surprised because she had originally believed in the equation, Friendship = Lots of Time Together. Now she and George see less of each other but enjoy a kind of quality time together.

In our mobile society, friendships and indeed marriages frequently must be carried on over great distances and with minimal face-to-face contact. Much to my surprise, friends' being physically unavailable to each other can have positive as well as the expected negative effects upon the experience of friendship. Some people said that infrequent contact made their time together *more* valuable and easier because they had more to share at each meeting. Boredom was less a possibility and they felt less burdened by demands on each other than they would experience on a day-to-day basis. One woman mentioned that with the distance and time between her and a friend she was more easily able to make the friendship strong "in her mind." She said that even though being together was important, feeling close was more within her control.

**Modularized Friendship.** Another way in which ideal friendships are different from actual friendships is in the way the friendship is put together. While people feel that ideal friendship requires a package of attributes like trust, similarities, shared activities, and acceptance, *actual* relationships only realize a part of what is seen as ideal. That is, when asked to describe friendship, most participants recited a list of two to six components that they felt were necessary. However, those friendships in which they actually were engaged were clearly different: they included only parts of the full "ideal friendship." For example, June, who said that a very important part of friendship would be "sharing interests" nevertheless continued her contact with her friend Betty despite the fact that Betty had "changed so much I could hardly recognize her or think of what to say. I guess we're friends of habit."

**Friendships Are Rarely Abandoned.** Among the people I interviewed, most did not intentionally abandon a friendship. More commonly, if the relationship was not entirely satisfactory, they would either simply let it drift away or accept fragments of the prior friendship. But when asked about what would cause them to actively abandon a friendship (similar to uncoupling) people's answers were complex. Tyron said that he had clearly bailed out on friendships several times because he felt that the person involved was excessively negative or excessively dependent. He never explained to them the reasons he backed off, but just walked away.

Steve is a successful consultant who has been divorced for four years. After initially saying that it would be difficult to think of a reason for abandoning a friendship he suddenly remembered his lack of faith in a friend and how that led to their falling out:

*There was a woman friend of mine that I must admit I intentionally don't see anymore. The problem was that she was acting in a very dishonorable way. She was changing before my eyes into a superficial person who was just using her husband (who was quite a bit older than her) to get material things. Not only was I mad at her but I realized that we didn't have much to say to each other anymore.*

Some people said that the loss of trust would be the main reason that they would give up a friendship, but few actually followed through on this principle and actively abandoned a relationship. Emily, a forty-year-old real estate broker said that she would break off any relationship in which she was betrayed or lied to. Later on, though, it became quite clear that she maintained relationships with several women friends who had broken her trust. They had done so in such devastating ways as seducing Emily's lover away from her. Asked about her inconsistency she said, "I know I should let her go but somehow we keep hooking back into a relationship."

In addition to these active reasons for abandoning a friendship, several people said that some of their friendships just seemed to dissolve before their eyes. Seemingly both parties had come to the realization that they had little to connect them to each other.

**Relative Honesty.** Another way in which the relationships which people described as friendship were different from their abstract definitions was that the ideal of honesty as an important ingredient in friendships was enacted in the actual relationships as a kind of *relative* honesty. That is, they would often withhold things from their friends for a variety of reasons. This was quite different from their original description of friendships as utterly honest. Perhaps related to this enacting of relative honesty was the relative importance of trust and the way in which trust was managed in a relationship.

**Relative Trust.** Very often, as with honesty, the extension of trust in the relationships varied from person to person. The trust offered regarding delicate and personal parts of their lives was very different depending upon the person and the situation. In fact, as each participant discussed his or her network of friends it became clear that each friend played a different role in terms of the type and amount of trust invested in him or her. Some were trusted as friends with whom to talk about serious and painful topics; other friends were trusted and held close mainly for the kinds of support they might offer, whether it was financial, emotional, physical, or spiritual.

## Friendships after the Breakup: From A to Z

The tremendous variety of types of friendships is testimony to the seemingly boundless potential of human relationships. I have found a continuity of renewed and redefined intimacy balanced with a striving for personal growth in many of the couples I talked with, and that is indeed inspiring!

The friendships took the shape of everything from biannual casual phone calls to intensely entwined associations of family and friends. The variety of relationships will be laid out here through descriptions of life-style, behavior, and feelings of six distinct categories of relationships.[2]

### New Contact After Many Years

Eleanor, a fifty-year-old physical therapist, had recently met for the first time with her ex-husband, Ed, whom she had divorced some ten years earlier. After having thought little about Ed for those ten years—she has been raising a new family—she was very surprised to see him at the theater. She found herself drawn toward him with an odd kind of openness; they agreed to meet for lunch.

Eleanor and Ed were married for eleven years. For both, the

divorce process was difficult. They struggled frequently over a plethora of differences. Ultimately, in spite of a bevy of ambivalent feelings, Eleanor decided to make the break. Ed, who was only marginally aware that there was a real problem, was stunned by her decision to seek a divorce. Their divorce occurred in quite a different historical era, when divorce meant mutual hate, and because they had no children between them, Ed and Eleanor simply went their own separate ways and never saw each other in the interim.

Following this first reunion, Eleanor said that she was surprised by her own desire to know much more about him. As she looked across the table at him, she realized that she had forgotten feelings and thoughts not only about Ed, but about his family and her relationships with each of its members. Lots of questions lay unanswered. She said she wanted to know more:

*What did you do? What have you done for the last ten years? What ever happened to that lady you were involved with?* [*she wanted to know*] *And then when we split up, I lost all of his family whom I knew really intimately. His parents and brothers and sisters. And the minute we split I lost all those people. And all those friendships. It was finding out about all of them. Who was dead and who was alive. It meant more than I thought it would.*

She said that Ed seemed not to have changed from the time she last saw him. She wanted to somehow maintain contact with him, but her decision to divorce was reaffirmed to her as the right one. She didn't want to call Ed a good friend yet. Ed could offer her a large pool of memory about herself and their relationship which may have otherwise evaporated. She found it useful and comforting to fill in some of the gaps that she missed.

At this moment Eleanor was still not certain what kind of a relationship she would like to have with Ed. She felt uncertain about the consequences of reconnecting with him. She recognized that she would need the full consent and participation of her current husband, Al. In addition to her concern about Al's feelings, she was also concerned about her children and how they might feel getting to know the man to whom she was married so many years before their birth. In short, there were so many questions and ambiguities and yet so many possibilities that she needed time to consider which path she would choose.

## Friends in Need

Zack, now a college administrator, met Teresa when he was sixteen. They were both in high school and quickly became sweethearts. While they have maintained a rather tenuous contact over the years, Zack said that he had never lost his feeling of concern for her and couldn't even remember the specifics about why they had uncoupled.

Even though he has no doubts that he continues to consider Teresa his friend, he is still left in a quandary about what kind of friendship they share:

*My relationship with Teresa is hard to describe. We were high school sweethearts but when I left for college we just lost track of each other. Then about three years ago she called me saying that she had moved to the area but was having a real difficult time. She was struggling with one relationship problem after another and was out of control with alcohol. I felt concerned and tried to talk with her but I must admit that I was worried about what my involvement with her would mean for the rest of my life. Anyway, last year her latest boyfriend called and said that he thought I might be able to help. With great anxiety I agreed to try to help him get her into a treatment program. It seems to have paid off. I heard from her just the other day and she seems much more in control. I don't know if this is considered friendship or not but I will probably always care about her.*

Despite the ambiguity that Zack mentioned, throughout our conversation he repeatedly remarked that he is aware that his continued friendship with Teresa adds to the quality of his life as a whole.

## Occasional Calls and Dinner in the City, Just for Two

Joan, a thirty-six-year-old physical therapist currently living in Colorado, and John, an advertising executive living in the East, got together ten years ago. They agreed that their relationship as a couple was characterized by a good feeling of friendship, a remarkable intellectual excitement, good sex, and a persistent feeling of being accepted "for who we were." Joan initiated a breakup because she was overwhelmed at the death of her father and felt a strong urge to be with her family who lived in another state. Because of her strong relationship with her father Joan was cast adrift in depression and profound despair at his loss.

*It was a very confusing time. It felt like I was losing control of me. John escalated on me in the hardest way. He was being very helpful and wanted me to stay and be there with him. The problem was that I was feeling more depressed and pulling into myself. I really didn't know what I was doing.*

Aware of the weakness of her boundaries—her ability to operate as a separate individual—Joan felt the need for a significant period of almost total separation from John following her decision to leave the relationship. This was so despite the fact that he was a person whom she knew she still cared for deeply.

After John helped her pack her things and leave for her family, the two maintained only minimal and quite superficial contact by telephone for the next year.

As the situation with her family and the death of her father was resolved, Joan and John, on the spur of the moment, enjoyed a meeting for dinner on one of Joan's visits back to her old haunts. It was clear to both of them that much water had gone under the bridge; they held no real expectation that they might get back together as a couple. John was in a new relationship and Joan was becoming settled and happy in her new home in the West. As they talked they recognized that they shared much because of their brief history as a couple and affirmed that they did not want to lose touch.

Because they both lead active lives—John with his career and new family, Joan with new romantic attachments and her own career—and because they live two thousand miles apart the friendship which they have constructed is limited by time constraints. Nonetheless, their friendship is meaningfully supported by telephone calls every few months and dinner when one or the other traverses the continent. When they get together they both feel as though little time has passed. They share an abiding appreciation and love of the shared history they enjoyed and a genuine consistent desire to stay current in knowledge of what's happening with the other. As Joan said:

*I really want to know about his life and I want him to know about mine. I know that he knows me in a way that few others know me.*

*It's important even though we are in different parts of the country. There's a feeling of caring and an acceptance of the other person and who they are. It's been years since I've seen him but when we were talking on the phone last week it's as if we were together yesterday.*

Who knows what would have happened if Joan had not been confronted with the difficult life challenges which led to her separation from John. What is clear is that she was grateful to have John remain in her life as a caring friend.

## Ex-Lovers, Business Partners, and Still Friends

Many places of employment have policies against employees becoming romantically involved with each other. The reasons for these policies range from concern about favoritism to a well-worn pessimism about how individuals will cope with a relationship that doesn't work out, and fears of the resultant impact on job performance and general employee morale.

Given this common assumption about the difficulty of working together, becoming lovers, breaking up, and then remaining friends, perhaps one of the most impressive types of couples that I interviewed were those who remained friends despite being ex-lovers or ex-spouses *and* business partners as well. These relationships add texture to the ex-lovers-as-friends mosaic.

Steve and Diane, both in their late twenties when they met, got together when they both arrived as junior partners in a consulting firm. Steve had just moved from the South and into the firm at the invitation of the senior partners. Diane was in the process of breaking up with another lover. Both of them reported that the intellectual compatibility and chemical excitement between them fueled a rapid coupling between them. Because they were working on a joint project, they began spending long hours together in the office and in the field. Steve, who had been previously married to a woman who he felt was very understated and quite depressed, was swept off his feet by their ability to work and play together without confusing or damaging one another or themselves.

Through an unusual set of circumstances, Steve and Diane simultaneously moved from positions of junior partnership in the firm to primary leadership and found themselves parenting a new organization. Six months later they were married with much excitement and with fond approval from their friends and employees. Being the bosses had its privileges.

One year later by mutual agreement Diane took on a project that required frequent travel to another country. Partly because of the pressures of their jobs and the estrangement of their frequent separations, both began to feel undernourished and resentful. Diane and Steve began an "I gotta leave, I want to leave, I don't know how to leave, let's fight about it" ritual. Despite their commitment to their couple relationship, after a year of couples therapy and much individual soul searching, they decided to throw in the towel on the marriage.

Despite the anger and resentment that had been building and which continued through the first year after their divorce, neither Steve nor Diane had any doubt that they wanted to stay friends after the initial pain was over. They wanted to maintain their friendship out of mutual respect, and of course, because they still had responsibilities as parents of their organization.

Both Steve and Diane describe that first year as one of the worst of their lives as they tried to juggle their business relationship, their dying marriage, and their fledgling friendship. After they both became involved with new partners, the furor began to settle down.

Looking back on their experience, they remarked that one of the most difficult aspects of making the transition to a new relationship came in trying to convince their colleagues that it could be done and that the organization would survive the pain. In the second and third year following their divorce, Steve and Diane progressively began to use each other as important confidants and colleagues, entrusting each other with most intimate concerns in their lives. While neither felt any pressing necessity to share with current partners the details and history of their breakup, neither were they reluctant to answer any questions that their new partners might have. I will discuss this issue of sharing information with new partners in chapter six.

▼

Currently, six years since their divorce, both Steve and Diane still manage the same business and are living more separate lives. They are less intensely engaged than they were two or three years ago. They more often communicate around necessary business matters. They have aligned themselves elsewhere in other relationships and family and have less time and opportunity to cultivate their friendship, but still say that maintaining their friendship is one of the proudest acts of their lives.

A business/friendship relationship which followed a path quite different from Steve and Diane's is that of Marie and Joel. Marie met Joel on a business project. Despite the fact that she was still in a twenty-year marriage, she got involved with him. Her emotional divorce occurred ten years before because of her husband's alcoholism, but she remained married and living together in the interests of the family and children.

After about a year of working and sharing many weekends and evenings together, Marie and Joel began to identify themselves as a couple and went public with their relationship. Joel was a fine companion with humor and intellect; their relationship offered what Marie described as "good sex." He was well liked by Marie's children.

Two years later, Joel, who had been struggling for many years with severe depression, began to find great comfort from a new self-help, quasi-religious organization. While many areas of their relationship remained strong and engaging, Marie said that she could no longer tolerate Joel's involvement in this self-help organization because of the strong imposing moral philosophy that it embraced. She had begun to lose respect to some degree for Joel because of his participation in the organization. Marie said that working together in the same company business was problematic only because as they began their transition from coupledom it was emotionally difficult to see each other on a daily basis. It took perhaps four months for them to sort out their relationship and to emerge in a new relationship characterized as friendship without the coupled commitment and identification.

Unlike Steve and Diane, Marie and Joel have continued a close association and have considerable contact between themselves and other members of their social networks. For example, Marie was proud of herself in the past year for introducing Joel to her current boyfriend. "They are very much alike; they seem to have a good relationship and enjoy a very good time together as golf buddies and tennis buddies," she said. Marie, her new partner, her ex-partner, and his new wife frequently spend time as a foursome, enjoying themselves immensely together at a lake cabin.

Marie and Joel's relationship never was a real commitment for either of them, so their breakup was not so difficult to endure. It is still important to recognize the great pleasure they enjoy from continuing on as friends even though their relationship "didn't go anywhere," as they put it.

## Close Friends/Network of Family Life Relationships
Chris and Mike had been involved with each other on and off for about five years. While they had, and still have, a mutually respectful and caring relationship they seemed to always be in different developmental stages in their lives. Chris was invested in both raising her children and her career; Mike, a longtime bachelor and confirmed nonparent, was heavily invested in both his career and music. Mike wanted to be free to immerse himself in the growing complexities of the music industry while Chris was committed to being an available parent. These differences ultimately precluded maintaining a committed mated relationship but because there was so much caring and shared history, Chris

and Mike opted to retain their relationship in the form of a close friendship.

One of the external factors that supported their post-breakup friendship in some form, was that Chris and Mike were both integral parts of a family-like friendship network. In addition to maintaining the continuity of their relationship through getting together for dinner or walks on the beach, they also achieved continuity through gatherings of friends, where they each felt entirely comfortable introducing the other to current partners. Says Chris,

*I got involved with Mike in the first place because he was a wonderful human being. I can't imagine his not being a part of my life just because we're not a couple. I also can't imagine not supporting anything or anyone that would contribute to Mike's happiness.*

In addition to her feeling towards Mike as an individual Chris said that each was also motivated to maintain their friendship because of their shared network of friends.

*While I truly believe that we would have chosen friendship anyway, our mutual friends—actually, it's more like a family of choice—means a great deal to each of us. We enjoy being together both by ourselves and in the context of our friends. Usually these gatherings also include our current partners. As a matter of fact both Mike and my current partner are friends in their own right and the lady that Mike is with now is someone that I look forward to knowing better and welcoming into our family.*

I was impressed by the way Chris and Mike were able to maintain a very high level of intimacy throughout the twists and turns of their relationship in its many forms. Chris and Mike each worked diligently throughout the life of their relationship, and into the present to maintain clarity about "whose neurotic stuff was whose." The persevering feeling of caring they continue to share is testimony to the higher level of purpose they both feel in knowing one another.

Shiloh and Fredrico are another couple who divorced but stayed tightly connected within their extended network of friends.

They met and quickly became involved with each other in the midst of many life changes for both of them. Shiloh was still in the throes of deciding whether or not to stay in a marriage to a man with whom she did *not* want to maintain friendship. Otherwise, she was buoyed by a successful, exciting career as a nutritional expert. Fredrico, also meeting success in many areas, was living a more tenuous emotional life.

Their period together was filled with humor and liveliness, but ultimately Shiloh initiated a divorce process that was painful and complex. She decided to give up their marriage because she believed that Fredrico's abuse of drugs and his related social failures, such as not showing up even for parties *they* were hosting, were not going to change. There were other seemingly unchangeable and disabling differences between them as well. Their separation was also in part caused by their spending much time each year separated from each other, with little opportunity to work through their differences.

Like Chris and Mike, Shiloh and Fredrico continued to be good friends, strongly supported by their network of family and friends. And like several other participants in the study, Fredrico and Shiloh's new husband have become good friends as well. What is extraordinary about this relationship is that the friendship between Fredrico and Shiloh's current husband has actually taken on a life of its own, independent of their shared relationship with Shiloh.

## Part of the Family

Elizabeth and Rex met over twenty-five years ago when Rex was a student at the university and Elizabeth was still in high school. For the first three years that they knew each other, their relationship was intense on several levels but was nonsexual. Pointing to these other levels of important relatedness, Elizabeth said, "When I met him I knew I knew him. There was a kind of instant recognition. I knew he would make a good mate. It was like we were sort of meant to be together." As she describes it, an important part of their relationship while they were together was her sense of being able to grow with Rex. She felt he helped her and encouraged her to be herself and explore new areas of her life. It was three years before they had a sexual relationship, but in that three-year period, they spent several hours together daily enthralled in deep intellectual and spiritual sharing.

Elizabeth remembers that at the beginning her expectations of the relationship were great; she hoped that they would marry, spend their lives together, never be bored, not feel too possessive of each other, and yet have a great sense of involvement, which would include having children.

Soon after they began their sexual relationship, Elizabeth became pregnant. She withheld this information from Rex for some time fearing that he would react poorly to the news. Apparently, she was right. When she told him she was pregnant, he responded by saying that he felt trapped. At that point Elizabeth made the decision not to insist that they remain together. In fact, she insisted that they separate so that Rex could go his way and achieve his life goals.

While it was not quite as clear for Rex, for Elizabeth it was important to remain in contact, not only because they shared a child together, which she would then go on to raise, but also because she felt a continuing connection to Rex that she couldn't quite identify. Throughout the last twenty-five years, they have at different times moved closer and further apart. Throughout most of this period Elizabeth had considered that their relationship was essentially a friendship, and was unconscious of her own hope that they would reunite as a couple at some point. As I will describe elsewhere in this book, Elizabeth for over twenty-five years failed to recognize that she had not in fact given up on the romantic element of this relationship, but had to some extent deluded herself into believing that they were living a "life of friendship."

Two years ago, after a friend pointed out that Elizabeth had been carrying a torch for Rex for all these years, she realized that she had to come to terms with the fact that they would never be a couple again. Her failure to let go of the relationship fantasy had already had a negative impact on a series of relationships that Elizabeth had engaged in over those past twenty-five years. She currently believes that her unconscious belief that she and Rex would ultimately reunite led her to choose to be involved with a "string of alcoholic, abusing losers," a situation that inevitably left her periodically available for a new chance at a relationship with Rex.

Elizabeth's new awareness brought some interesting results. First, she said "it was as though I had come out of a fog." She felt freed and soon moved onto a new relationship that grew into her current marriage. This new marriage was less filled with pain and even joyful. The abuse that accompanied alcoholism and constant mutual disappointment that had been a consistent part of the other relationship disasters was not present.

The second result of her decision to stop carrying the torch for Rex was that indeed for the first time they *did* become friends! Since that time Rex has become increasingly involved with Elizabeth's family, including her relationship with her husband and his own son with Elizabeth. He attends many family activities, and is involved in much of the decision making and support of their son. Rex also has developed an independent relationship with Elizabeth's current husband, which they both find very rewarding.

## Analysis for Support and Inspiration

If as you struggle and glide through breakup and transition, you feel as though you are trying to balance a stack of glasses while staying afoot in a spinning room filled with loose ball bearings, take heart. Remember that in each of the relationships just described complications are the rule rather than the exception.

**Complexity.** These six briefly described friendships are each marked by a consistent complexity. We have explored only the outward behavior and superficial emotions involved in forming viable friendship after a breakup of a couple relationship. As you attempt to create your own friendship, remember that beneath the behavior and emotions lies an intricate balance of physical, psychological, emotional, social, and spiritual needs, not only for the ex-partners but of those around them as well. Remember how complex these successfully shifted situations really are as you go through a process you may find overwhelming and disheartening.

**Change as Consistent.** The new friendship which rises out of the ashes of uncoupling continually changes. Every aspect of living persistently pulls the friendship in different directions. What you work out today may be obsolete tomorrow. As Elizabeth mused,

*Our way of relating to each other has changed a lot since the beginning. We have been lovers, pen pals, counselors, and have at times even just forgotten that our relationship existed. Things just keep on changing.*

▼

The perhaps less obvious implication of the fact of change is that when you attempt to understand and to effect a positive transition, it is important to remember that the process of the change—the *way* you make the changes—is as important as the content of the relationship, or even more so. Focus on communication, interaction patterns, and open models of relatedness.

**Uniqueness.** Friendships differ not only from couple to couple, but for each person within the relationship. While this may restate the obvious, it is an important truth to remember as you attempt to build your new friendship.

As you struggle to maintain your postbreakup friendship you may find yourself frustrated by the lack of relevant signs to guide you. In the early stages of couples therapy the reality of the uniqueness of each relationship is often a source of great frustration. People come to therapy wanting to be given *the* correct, successful way to relate. But there is no model relationship or way of being together as a couple. As couples understand their differences and accept them and as commonalties of purpose emerge, this same uniqueness brings the couple a sense of freedom and pride of accomplishment.

## Ex-Lover/New Lover Friendships

Though I am loath to attempt to define *the* "healthy" relationship —whether as a couple or as ex-partners—the people I interviewed said that they felt most comfortable when they achieved a flowing, supportive balance among the needs of each ex-partner, the postbreakup friendship, and the new couple relationships that followed. Further, in the relationships that seemed to be the most healthy a special friendship frequently emerged between ex-partners and new lovers. This was true for both men and women. I found this to be particularly remarkable among the men because men's friendships are often described as rather detached, activity focused, and competitive. These men did not at all meet this stereotype.

The important thing is that each person's connection with an ex-partner or partners is unique. This presents a challenge not only to the individuals involved, but to me as a psychotherapist. I am constantly reminded of my limitations in applying the experience of one client to that of another. To some extent you must find solutions of your own for problems of your own, understanding that you and your friend/ex-lover have limitless possibilities for a gratifying relationship, unbounded by social convention or the experience of others.

## Breakups That Didn't End in Friendship
Several of the people I interviewed mentioned that there were some relationships in their past that they *did not* attempt to transform into friendships. The following tendencies can contribute to breakups and prevent the viability of lasting friendships after the breakup:

1. being judgmental
2. prolonging the breakup process, allowing the tension level to get too high
3. indecisiveness, continual waffling back and forth
4. the inability of the couple to agree on where the fault lies
5. dishonesty
6. triangulation, or getting someone else in the middle of the breakup, such as a family member or friend
7. poor handling of property distribution
8. excessive blaming

CHAPTER

# 3

# THE BENEFITS OF REMAINING FRIENDS:
## With our intimate relationship dissolved, why *should* we remain friends?

▼

1. What would make you want to maintain a friendship after the breakup?
2. What aspects of your ex-partner or the relationship do you miss most?
3. What would you hope to get for yourself out of the new friendship?
4. What unfinished business remains between you and your ex-partner?
5. What do you need to learn from your ex-partner that will improve your chances for a better relationship next time?
6. What kind of relationship would you like to maintain with your ex-partner? What would you like to do together? talk about? How much time would you want to spend together?

The benefits of remaining friends with former lovers are as varied as the relationships. Even when you don't choose to continue living with your partner, there are many aspects of that

▼

person and their way of relating that form the basis of your desire to be friends. Your partner, for example, may have had a certain way of listening which made you feel truly understood. Perhaps he used humor in a way that added delightful spice to your life. Maybe she was a trusted professional colleague, or he was an extraordinary chef. You experienced deep emotional bonds together. For many, unconditional love endures and enriches their lives when the conditional nature of the relationship makes living together out of the question. Understanding these two ways of being with someone facilitates understanding of the ways in which you can benefit from maintaining friendship after the breakup.

John Welwood in his book *Challenge of the Heart* offers a useful clarification of the differences between conditional and unconditional love. Conditional love, he says, is related to the "form" of the relationship that you have with someone. That is, conditional love is dependent upon how well our partner meets our needs, desires, and personal considerations. Does he like the kind of music you like? Is she sufficiently altruistic? Do you want the same amount of sexual contact? These kinds of questions are evidence of the kind of conditions we put on love.

Thomas and Eileen decided to separate as a couple because aspects of their daily life were chronically out of sync. Thomas wakes early, ready to roll. Eileen needs to sleep in whenever possible. Thomas felt a desire to be sexual no more than twice a week, and Eileen felt hurt and rejected each time Thomas declined her sexual initiations. The combination of these and other persistent differences contributed to their decision to break up. Nevertheless, each clearly acknowledged that these conditional aspects of their relationship were differences of personal desire and not failures of obligation or signs of pathology.

Unconditional love, on the other hand, does not pay attention to what is similar or what matches between two people but is rather a less limited appreciation of others simply for who they are in the world. Unconditional love reaches above reason and may be experienced as a kind of "being with" the other person.[1]

Megan, an advertising executive, put it this way:

*I didn't have to be anything. I could just be me. Since we are not involved we can talk more openly. I asked him the other day "How's your sex life?" Even though it was a serious problem in our relationship I had no difficulty asking him about it at that time because I was in neutral.*

In looking at these two kinds of loving, it is perhaps easier to see why two people might say that they love one another but nevertheless do not want to be a couple and live together. Taking these two forms of love into account also makes it easier to understand the hidden basis for friendship after the breakup. Each person I interviewed expressed some awareness of this difference and an abiding unconditional love for their ex-partner.

The notion that there are many kinds of love is in itself important, and helpful for making your transition. Differences in life-style, attitude, behavior, or career goals, may be sufficient grounds for a parting of the ways. But for the sake of the friendship and for the individuals involved, where an unconditional, enduring love exists it is important that it not be denied or destroyed by misunderstanding. But these two approaches to understanding the meaning of love are but two ways of looking at the issue. Many others are possible and should be explored to help the transition process and achieve the many benefits gained when lost lovers turn friends.

Megan, with some sadness but clear conviction, put it this way:

*Because I wanted children at a time when the clock was running out,*
*and he didn't, we had to split up. It was one of those immovable*
*differences. But that doesn't mean that I don't still care about him.*

To some extent your attitudes as individuals and your place
in the process of transition will play a role in the type of benefits
you can gain from your effort to remain friends. An important
part of your attitude is the way in which you look at your world
of relationships. Further, your view of this world depends upon
what you have been exposed to and what you have allowed
yourself to believe or accept as valuable information. With this
in mind, a major purpose of this chapter will be to expose you to
new perspectives in loving.

To become aware of benefits available, complete the following exercise. The exercise places you into a very relaxed state of
receptivity and suggests to your unconscious mind that you be
open to new ideas. Variations of this procedure may be found in
many books on relaxation, self-hypnosis, and peak performance.
Some are listed at the back of this book.

## Relaxation and Receptivity Exercise

**1.** Find a quiet, comfortable place to sit where you will not
be disturbed for about fifteen minutes.

**2.** While sitting or lying in a comfortable position close
your eyes and take ten slow, deep breaths. As you breathe in,
breathe the air all the way down into your stomach.

**3.** As you breathe in and out, say to yourself, "I am relax-
ing. I am taking this time to relax for myself. I am feeling more
and more relaxed." Notice that with each breath your body will

begin to feel more relaxed, perhaps heavier and more firmly settled in the chair.

**4.** As you reach the tenth breath (or when you feel truly more relaxed) slowly return to your normal rate of breathing.

**5.** With your eyes still closed, imagine that in the center of your head there is a soft, white, glowing light. Focus your attention on that light and allow yourself to drift into it.

**6.** After a few minutes, imagine that you are walking through the light to a place that is very peaceful for you; a place that either you remember or can imagine will be a place in which you will feel very comfortable.

**7.** When you reach this special place in your mind, whether it be a beach, a mountain hideaway, or any place that reminds you of peaceful, warm comfort, look around at what or who is there and feel yourself becoming more and more comfortable.

**8.** Now, after a short while say to yourself, "I am at peace. I feel comfortable and warm. I am ready to receive new ideas, new dreams."

**9.** Stay with your thoughts of being receptive for a few minutes and then slowly begin to return to your waking state with your eyes open.

**10.** When you are ready, open your eyes and take a deep breath.

**11.** Take a few moments to reorient yourself to your surroundings, perhaps go for a short walk. When you return, begin reading again.

I encourage you to use this exercise as often as you wish.

## Some Benefits of Remaining Friends

Each person I interviewed mentioned at least several of the following benefits of remaining friends after they broke up.

1. A warm sense of deep, enduring intimate connection
2. A special and helpful knowledge of each other
3. Forgiving the other, which helps you forgive yourself
4. Stability and continuity of being cared for
5. The value of shared history
6. An opportunity to work through differences without the threat of breakup
7. A chance to grow, working through psychological and emotional distortions
8. Simple relaxed companionship
9. Pride of accomplishment
10. The psychological and physical health benefits that come with having an ongoing, secure social support network

## Warm Sense of Deep, Enduring, "Intimate" Connection

*There is still and always will be a deep connectedness with us. He's in my dreams sometimes. I know I would be silly to lose him from my life.*

Contrary to the stereotype of warring divorcees, the men and women I interviewed said that one of the most important benefits of actively maintaining their friendship after the breakup was the continuing warm feeling that they knew each other in a very intimate way. In fact, many mentioned that rather than decreasing, their feelings of intimacy *increased* after separation and divorce. This idea, that intimacy would increase after breakup, seems contrary to what most people would expect. How can it be?

Before responding to this question, let me define the word *intimacy*. One psychologist defines intimacy as a "sharing of activity and expression resulting in a sense of knowing the other (person) beyond the level of statuses and roles characteristic of public life."[2] I would add to this definition that intimacy involves a kind of emotional openness and availability to the other person that we do not share with others.

The essential components are:

1. Some kind of sharing (activities or communication)
2. A kind of knowing of each other which goes beyond what we see on the surface
3. An emotional openness and availability not shared with others

Though the presence of all of these characteristics in a relationship will increase feelings of intimacy, each independently contributes separately to that feeling. Joan, a physical therapist, defines an intimate relationship here in her own terms:

*It's important [that we be friends] even though we are in different parts of the country. There's a sure feeling of caring and an acceptance of the other person and who they are. It's been years since I've seen him but when we were talking on the phone last week it's as if we were together yesterday.*

The notion that the more "coupled" people are, the more intimate they will naturally be is a myth. While two people may indeed become more familiar with each other as they spend more time together, they do not necessarily become more intimate. In fact, much recent research has indicated that couples often tend to become less intimate with each other as time passes and they become more coupled.[3]

This decrease in intimacy most often occurs because they

gradually stop communicating with each other and consequently stop seeing each other as whole persons made up of emotional, psychological, physical, and spiritual aspects. They are instead lulled into believing they know each other through the monotony of daily routines.

Barbara and Jim found themselves in my office after another in a series of fights that had been erupting with increased frequency over the past year. In a fit of anger he swore to Barbara that he would leave the relationship "if you don't listen to me!" In the session we learned that both Jim and Barbara were committed to one life activity or another at least seventy hours per week. Recently, the only time they had spoken to each other was to give information about household activities like the kid's schedules, bills, and maintenance problems, or when they were fighting.

In the last twenty minutes of the session, I suggested that they take the remaining time to share with each other one event, feeling, or thought that was important to them which had occurred in the past week. After repeating for ten minutes that he could not think of anything important, except that he was terribly bored with his life, a tear rolled from his eye. "I can't think of anything that is special to me. What's worse I can't think of anything that Barbara has said to me that is important for her. I don't know either of us anymore!"

Of course, not all couples succumb to these pressures. There are those who somehow anticipate the deadening effect of the structure and routine in married life and consciously inject intimate contacts into their day-to-day living. Much of the "relationship" literature being written today actually focuses upon the ways in which couples can maintain intimate relatedness in the face of modern fact and myth.

Jack and Denise seem to have anticipated these potential

deadening effects of everyday life even before they got married. Living a very full life in an eastern city with their two children, two careers, and two cars certainly would seem to offer much opportunity for movement away from each other into estrangement, misunderstandings, and decreased intimacy. On the advice of the local priest, Jack and Denise included as part of their wedding vows that they would spend at least one weekend a month away by themselves. They were to focus their conversations at these times mainly on issues that were intimately important to them. They agreed that during these times they would not discuss day-to-day struggles and difficulties in enacting their roles as parents, husband and wife, and employees. Also in their vows was a promise that if either should begin to feel distant from the other, or if one began to distrust the other for any reason, and if such issues were not being remedied by their own conversation, they would call in a counselor to help them bridge the gap. As a further affirmation of their desire to remain together, they decided that they would work together on some type of project throughout their married life. Since their decision, they have read books, written stories, and published a book together, and have taken on a variety of other projects as their way of offering themselves time to work on something together.

These misunderstandings about intimacy which affect couple life also clearly influence our beliefs about the transition to friendship after the breakup. Isolina Ricci in her otherwise very valuable book, *Mom's House, Dad's House*, insists that when couples break up they must face the fact that "Successfully ending a divorce means moving away from intimacy."[4] If you believe this entirely, transitioning to friendship will indeed be difficult if not meaningless.

While it may be true that when you become separated or divorced you will be less involved in some aspects of each other's lives, this does not mean that you must give up an abiding sense of contact and closeness. As a matter of fact, ex-partners commonly decrease their involvement in those aspects of their lives which could actually detract from a feeling of intimacy, such as sharing household routines, and this makes them more available for other aspects of relatedness that are more conducive to intimacy, such as talking about their own struggles in the world. When I asked both my clients and interviewees to define "friendship," some aspect of the experience of intimacy, as I have defined it, was always an ingredient.

Jody, thirty-five-year-old community organizer, attended a lecture on the process of divorce at a local community college. The instructor described all the aspects of the couple relationship that would change following a divorce, e.g., sharing laundry, sharing expenses, making joint decisions, balancing their childcare needs, and a variety of others. As she listened to his comments she realized that if all those aspects of her life with her husband changed and they were living separately, they would be freed up to talk about things that were actually more important to them. They could talk openly about her fears regarding her husband's financial risk taking, her worries about growing old, and his struggle to define himself without reference to his family.

An important result of keeping the warm sense of connection mentioned by so many of the clients I worked with is the feeling of total acceptance by the found friend. In one way or another their couple years—even the most intimate ones—were tainted with the fear of rejection or sanctioning for simply being themselves. But with their ex-partners turned friends it was different. They know all about each other, yet are unafraid that the other will abuse the knowledge or leave the relationship. They were *more free* to express parts of themselves that they tended to withhold from their partner. Joan, the physical therapist who left John when her father died, explained it this way:

> The thing that holds us as friends is the tremendous compatibility intellectually and playwise. That acceptance. We allowed for the change that occurred over the years. It's a person who can move with you [through life changes and development] over the years. I could see us being in the old people's home and we would still like each other as people. We still would have our same sense of humor and would be able to put up with each other's neuroses or whatever you want to call it. You know I can be pretty nuts and there are certain people that allow me the space for being that kind of outrageous and not judge me.

Our need to be intimate and our availability for intimacy with others may differ from month to month, day to day, or even from moment to moment. These variations result from each of our individual emotional and spiritual states as well as the social situations in which we find ourselves. In Joan's case, her lover was very attentive, caring, and emotionally involved with her not only when they were a couple but as they were breaking up. This quality of attention is still important to her in their continuing friendship and would be essential to any serious relationship she enters. However, immediately after they broke up she was so overwhelmed by her family issues, most specifically with the death of her father, that she couldn't bear her partner's attempts to be close or even to be helpful. Even though his attempts to be intimate and caring were what she might have wanted at another time, she did not have the energy or peace of mind to respond appropriately. In order to accept his attention she had to do too much screening of his affection, an action she did not have the energy to undertake.

> It was a very confusing time. It escalated on me. He escalated on me. He was being very helpful and wanting me to stay and be there with him.

*The problem was that I was feeling more depressed and pulling into myself.*

Paul and Kathy's friendship changed remarkably over the six years after their separation and divorce. After the fifth year of their marriage, Kathy became involved in a relationship with another man. After a painful internal struggle, she decided that she wanted to leave Paul. Even though she did not understand her reasons as clearly as she would have liked, she knew, at least, that being with Paul always left her feeling alone and unfulfilled. She did not care that her new relationship might turn out to be only an illusion of the connection she longed for; she knew she had to follow her heart, though there was much she liked about Paul. She wanted to remain available as a friend but did not want to be married.

Paul felt rejected, angry, and hurt. Kathy's departure was a powerful blow to his self-esteem and consequently he felt that he did not want to communicate with her. He went about the business of trying to put it behind him. Nevertheless, over the next four years, they indeed communicated with each other, albeit about issues that were manageable; much cooler issues than those which fueled the breakup.

Over the six years since their divorce, Paul's intense feelings have somewhat worn off. He and Kathy frequently spend time together, going on long walks, sharing stories about their now separate lives. Paul pointed out that those small superficial contacts in the first years after their breakup were important because they maintained the connection between them. He believes that if they had not continued to communicate and to discuss the easier issues, the satisfying relationship that now exists between them would have been lost. Looking back, he recognizes that the time and the circumstances right after the breakup made him initially want to remain distant from Kathy, though these were not his true feelings toward her as a human being.

## You Each Have Special, Helpful Knowledge of the Other

Because couples share an intimate history, ex-couples invariably have a substantial special knowledge about each other's public and private selves. They know each other's private likes and dislikes, their deepest fears, their perhaps silly but entrenched habits of living, their behavior in relationships, etc. This special knowledge means that someone who knows you well can point out to you when you are repeating old, self-defeating patterns. In part, because you are no longer a couple, subject to the fear of breakup, you can offer this kind of feedback to each other with a believable sense of acceptance. Even your best same-sex friends do not know you as well as someone with whom you have lived.

As Megan points out, you don't have to worry about what your ex-partner might come to know; he or she knows it all!

*I think with ex-lovers there's lots more depth. Less vulnerability. What can you do wrong? They know all about you. They know me better and accept me more for who I am and what I am.*

Because your ex-partner knows you so well, with some caution you can assume that when you want to talk in depth about important issues, you needn't start at the beginning each time. I say "with caution" because assuming that others know the important facts about us when they actually don't is often a source of much unintended miscommunication.

Having another person know us so intimately can mean that, if we trust them, they can help us beyond giving advice in the often difficult task of understanding ourselves and our relationships with others. As Jean put it:

*In that I know he knows me so well I can trust that what he reflects back to me is the truth of who I am.*

And Betty found that she very much appreciated the chance to talk about her evolving relationships with her lover-turned-friend:

*He knows me like no one knows me. The other day we were talking about some problems I'm having in my current relationship. His response, with the welcome air of humor in his voice, was, "Betty, you're doing it again." And you know, he was right. I'm not sure I would have listened to anyone other than him saying the same thing.*

Your extensive special knowledge about another person also brings you closer to knowing them as a whole person. As anyone who has been in a relationship of any duration will tell you, the person we see at the office or at the market is but a fraction of the whole person. To really have special "whole person" knowledge about another takes a great deal of time and involvement through many situations. Thus, the person or persons with whom you have lived are unique in their knowledge of the larger you. Ironically, though we live a large portion of our lives with our birth families, even they are often not privy to our innermost concerns. Their understanding of who we are may be distorted or more distorted than others. Jean recognized this fact about families, reflecting,

*My family relationship is different. They know me in terms of intellectual thoughts and ideas on things. But it's not the same kind of intimacy as with a lover. They know you in a different, deeper way.*

Jean went on to make an important point about the knowledge that our friends and family have about us: they know you based on the time when they were with you. Your family knows you as "little Johnny," and in some ways fails to recognize that you have changed from your childhood. For example, while I was visiting my extended family last week, at least six of my cousins and uncles separately made playful jabs about the fact that I was no longer wearing the beard I had worn—against the family norm —for fifteen years. The extraordinary fact is I shaved my beard two years ago and I have been to several family functions since, only to receive the same treatment. It was as if my family could not accept that I had actually changed. They continue to see me as I was fifteen years ago.

The same tendency to maintain a dated view of you is often true for intimate partners that you left years ago, especially if you have not stayed in touch.

## Forgiving the Other Helps You Forgive Yourself

A major reason that ex-partners do not remain friends is that they don't recognize the mutual basis for the breakup. Often a couple's refusal to recognize that it takes two to tango follows from their tendency to either blame themselves or their ex-partner, giving out or taking on mountains of unnecessary guilt. When both partners accept the mutual responsibility for the breakup, each is more able to accept and forgive the ex-partner and him or herself as well.

Molly, a thirty-six-year-old schoolteacher, and Ted, a forty-year-old plumber, lived together for fourteen years. At the time of the breakup, the official reason that Molly felt the relationship collapsed was that Ted had become involved with another woman. Enraged by her sense of betrayal, and by encouragement from supposedly well-meaning friends, Molly was consumed by her anger and consistently refused to try to understand any of her role in the breakup of their relationship.

In a therapy session six months after Ted moved out, Molly

did recognize that she had contributed to the end of the relationship through her increased preoccupation with her teaching duties and her students' needs to the exclusion of Ted. She had allowed her job to overshadow her marriage. Ted had unconsciously begun to look outside his marriage to meet his needs.

Despite her new awareness of her part in the breakup, Molly continued to remain angry and unforgiving towards Ted. She accused him of failing to let her know when she was not being available enough for him. However, as time passed, she became increasingly aware of intense feelings of guilt about how she had abandoned Ted without intending to exclude him. She also felt guilty for continuing to be angry with him when she indeed at least consciously acknowledged her role in the breakup.

On the suggestion of her therapist, Molly mustered all of her strength and made the effort to forgive Ted for his part in the breakup of the relationship. She chose to forgive Ted to help her reduce anger she felt for him. Much to her surprise, however, the more important effect of forgiving him was that she began to feel some acceptance for *herself* and was able to forgive herself, as she so well described.

*By forgiving him and trying to keep him as a friend, I was able to have more sympathy and forgiveness for myself. I was much less hard on myself.*

By granting herself this forgiveness, she also made an enduring friendship more possible.

## Stability and Continuity of Being Cared For
In a society as mobile as ours, it is easy to lose the sense that others in our lives consistently care about us. People we care for

dearly are often here today and gone tomorrow. Though most people seem—at least superficially—adjusted to this parade of departures, I suspect that it produces in each of us an underlying sense of loss. And this sense of unacknowledged loss may be related to the widespread depression among adults and children alike in this country.

If we lose the feeling of being cared for, our self-esteem is likely to drop. If only for the sake of our self-esteem, we need continuity of both caring and being cared for.

And staying friends and in continuous caring contact allows us to finish processes that began while we were still with our ex-partners. As Megan remarked,

*Ray was in a job transition while we were together. I was helping him by connecting him with friends in the business, building his self-esteem and teaching him certain parts of this type of business. I still care about him and staying friends has made it possible for me to finish what I was doing. There are other parts of our lives that needed to be finished too.*

*Another example is when I was with Fred. At the time I personally was working on learning how to feel and talk about my emotions. I had been closed off all of my life. After we broke up it was important to continue to have Fred as the person I could talk to and practice staying in touch with my emotions. He validated me constantly for my feelings.*

None of my subjects exemplified these comments about the importance and meaning of being consistently, unconditionally loving more than Jeff.

*Even though we are not going to be together as a couple, by keeping her as a friend I know that someone cares about me and loves me unconditionally. There's a lot of strength and happiness in knowing that you are loved. I feel that with this sense of being loved comes a greater sense of self-esteem.*

A sense of being cared for and the resulting increased self-esteem both help to effect a positive transition in the old relationship and facilitate a healthy entry into a new intimate relationship.

A study by Keith Davis found "best friendships" more stable than either "spouse" or "lover" relationships, in part because of "greater concern about the possibility of the relationships breaking up, particularly among unmarried lovers."[5] Likewise we can guess that in a lovers-turned-friends relationship this kind of stability will be common and important.

## The Value of Shared History
Knowing and appreciating who we are now is based partly upon our knowledge and acceptance of our past. Validation by an ex-partner of important elements of our personal and interpersonal history can help significantly to fill in the gaps and strengthen our sense of who we are today. In addition to validating or giving shared meaning and value to your past experiences, ex-lovers can validate the growth and changes we make over time. As Jean said,

*Because our lives had moved to different sides of the country we talk on the phone often but see each other infrequently. When I saw him last we had a great talk. He was able to point out ways in which I had changed for the better that even I hadn't noticed. It gave me a great feeling. A free pat on the back.*

Frank had thought much about the value of his time together with his ex-partner:

*We have a shared history that I don't want to lose. Not only are the memories enjoyable but when I talk to her I know that I don't have to always start at the beginning and go through a long explanation.*

## Without the Threat of Breaking Up, Differences Can Be Worked Through

Differences between a couple can be a source of great pleasure or pain. They can be minor—maybe you favor a different kind of music—or they can pose moral conflicts, as when you support different political parties, enjoy different sexual activities, or practice different religions. Differences can prevent partners from having their needs and wants met, perhaps because of discrepancies in sexual desire or discrepancies in how clean you like to keep a house. While such differences *can* become the basis for the breakup, they more often remain minor pains in the neck that can be dealt with via negotiation.

The fact that there are differences between individuals in a couple can be a problem depending upon the meaning that the individuals place upon the fact. Couples often interpret differences to mean that

1. they probably aren't "meant" for each other;
2. one of them must be wrong (bad, stupid, inadequate, etc.),
3. they cannot understand each other—an interpretation which leads to anxiety and confusion.

Despite these ways in which differences can become a problem in relationships I have found that couples can use artful and caring communication and negotiation, combined with changes in perspective, to keep the relationship intact, and even to grow through communication on differences.

A major block to constructively coping with the substance of significant differences is the partners' fear that if they say something or try to handle the differences directly they will cause a breakup. To protect themselves from this possibility, partners often withhold communication.

The experience of Seth and Melanie shows how differences and the failure to communicate them can lead to the breakup of an otherwise valuable relationship. At the same time they represent an example of the way in which two people after the breakup can come to view these differences in a more constructive light.

Looking back on his situation, Seth knows now that when he married Melanie he had a very strong feeling that she was too good for him. She was beautiful, intelligent, an important member of a wide network of friends, and offered him a sense of being cared for that he had never experienced.

Seth began to withhold information which he felt revealed differences between them. In addition to his fear of losing the relationship, his withholding was a habit which grew out of his own experience, having been raised in a dysfunctional family. The basic rule in his family was that individual differences do not exist. This unwillingness to accept the value of being an individual and of being different from other family members is a significant aspect of dysfunctional family life.

Despite their conception of their marriage as a strong one based on honesty, Seth soon began to withhold thoughts, feelings, and behavior he thought would reveal differences between them. Without discussing it Melanie began to get the picture, and began to withhold communication from him as well about issues from the most inane to the most important.

After a while when they tried to have serious conversations each felt the other was taking rigid positions without apparent foundation. The behavior and attitude of each became increasingly incomprehensible to the other. Not only were their differences being avoided but they could not talk about having differences. They could not answer the question, "What's wrong with this picture?" In the face of the resulting confusion and upset, each was left to fill in the blanks alone by attempting to read the other person's mind. Once they took up the impossible task of mind reading they were off to the disaster races. Resentment and mistrust, the demon seeds of estrangement and breakup, soon followed. In what he now retrospectively sees was a reaction to his guilt for withholding and frustration over the incomprehensible situation, Seth left one morning without further discussion and did not return.

After many months of therapy in which Seth learned about his own fear of differences and with the threat of breakup over, he took a chance and called Melanie. Much to his surprise he felt little fear in talking about these once-frightening differences. Not only was there less fear, disappointment, and anxiety about whether or not each would get their needs met but once acknowledged, the differences did not take on the same old threatening meanings. Even though both agreed that too much had changed in their lives to get back together as a couple, they saw the differences for what they were, not as derogatory comments or direct threats to the relationship.

The cycle of estrangement could thus be broken because it was no longer fueled by fear of abandonment. When they are aware that differences are okay, ex-partners can emerge more honestly to be accepted or appreciated. Being accepted and even appreciated for your uniqueness can be a powerful path to building self-esteem and a general sense of well being. Margaret smiled wryly as she said:

*I know I don't ever want to live with him again. But with him so close and with the freedom to deal with him when I want to, I can work out problems I had with him that I know came from our relationship and from my past. I don't think I could do this with anyone else because no one else gets to me the way he does.*

▼

Megan, a thirty-five-year-old advertising executive, saw that working through differences with her ex-partner had benefits beyond clearing the way for their friendship.

*By learning to communicate with my ex-partner and working through our differences, it really helps my current relationships.*

Once you have had the experience of really appreciating someone for who they are and being appreciated and accepted for who you are, each new relationship you enter will be based upon this new foundation of greater self-esteem and acceptance.

## Chance to Grow, Working Through Psychological and Emotional Distortions

While I try to focus on the positive, I have to acknowledge that most relationships are to some extent built upon negative projections. Each individual has unrealistic expectations or projections of his or her partner. In a projection, one partner projects his or her own fears, anger, or worries onto the partner. For example, if Jane is contemplating leaving her relationship with Elliot but is feeling guilty about it, she might accuse him of wanting to leave her. One common unrealistic expectation is the belief that your partner can meet all of your sexual, emotional, psychological, and spiritual needs. These projections and unrealistic expectations emerge from our attempts to cope with feelings that are too hot for us to handle. As you might expect, the dashing of unrealistic expectations against the rocks of truth in the turbulent phases of disengaging often increases partners' tendency to protect themselves by projecting their concerns onto their partners.

Often unrealistic expectations cannot be effectively uncovered and dispensed with in the context of being a couple. Because they are so personally and interpersonally threatening, we fear the way in which they will be received. And knowledge of the other's most vulnerable needs can be a dangerous weapon in times of anger and resentment.

Sometimes people are simply unaware that their expectations are unrealistic. It may take their friends, the grind of repetitious disappointment, or their therapists to point them out.

After the breakup, once the partners have gained enough distance from each other physically and emotionally, projections can be seen as such, rather than a source of much conflict. Examining projections can enrich each person's understanding of themselves and the way in which they cope with difficult feelings.

After the breakup, when your self-esteem has been rebuilt, unrealistic expectations, too, may come to light. If your ex-partner has become a trusted friend, you may be open to acknowledging the unrealistic nature of some of your expectations and learn to cope more effectively with the uncomfortable feelings which lie beneath these expectations. Again this is possible only when trust remains in the aftermath of the breakup. If the breakup with your ex-partner is filled instead with noxious anger, resentment, and mistrust, you will certainly miss these opportunities for increased understanding and acceptance of yourself and your ex-partner. As one woman found,

*From my therapy I know that some of our difficulty was that I had problems with my father and I used my ex-partner to work them out. While we were a couple this was destructive and hurtful to both of us. But now we have a little more distance and safety with each other. Now when he says or does those things that remind me of my father, we talk about it. He's less defensive.*

When your ex-partner is less defensive he or she will certainly be more available to you as a friend who holds the unique position in your life as someone who can help you know yourself and change for the better.

## Simple Relaxed Companionship

It is difficult to feel relaxed with new people no matter how excited we are by their presence. With ex-partners we have the opportunity for very valuable respite from this difficult aspect of life. I wish I had a dime for every time that single adult clients report the extraordinary drain of energy they experience when trying to establish a relaxed feeling of companionship with new people in their lives.

Shiloh, a thirty-year-old nutritionist, expressed these sentiments about her ex-partner:

*He's someone that I can go to lunch or to a movie and be comfortable with. The pressure is off. You don't have to play old games. Even though I'm fairly straight with people, I still feel constricted when I meet new people.*

The opportunity to spend time with someone you don't have to put on any airs with is clearly one of the benefits of maintaining friendship after the romance is over. Many people say that conversations with ex-partners are not only pleasurable moments in themselves but leave them with a clearer idea of the way they would like to be with all the people they meet.

## Pride of Accomplishment Emerges

Carol Masheter, writing on postdivorce relationships, remarks that an important theme of the intensive interviews she conducted with divorced couples was that nearly all found a strong sense of pride and accomplishment in their personal growth and improved relationship with their ex-partners after the ravages of the breakup had subsided. Many people notice changes in their relationships in general, including new romantic relationships, because of what they learned from successfully struggling through their divorces and breakups. As one ex-partner-turned-friend noted,

*It feels good to know that I have done it. It gives me the belief that I can create much more of my life the way that I want it. It just makes me feel good that we did what many said would be impossible.*

## The Psychological and Physical Health Benefits of a Social Support Network

When a couple acrimoniously tear their relationship apart, they suffer not only the loss of each other but that of each others' friends and family as well. The relationships among friends and family are a most complex labyrinth of emotions, needs, interests, indebtedness, loyalties, resources, and history, that Shakespeare might have been able to comprehend, but most of us find bewildering. The contribution that our social and family interrelations make to our psychological and even physical well-being has been the focus of much research over the past twenty years. Considerable evidence both in the scientific literature and in the reports of my interviewees shows that mental and physical health are, indeed, enhanced by ongoing contact with a wide network of friends. If ex-partners remain friends they will benefit not only from their association, but from each other's families and independent friendship networks as well.

Research has shown that people with fewer friends in their network have many more psychological and physical health problems. In the past, many of these health problems have been mistakenly identified as linked to the separation of divorce or breakup itself, but they can be more correctly seen as a result of the *way* in which people separate.

# 4

# WHEN EX-LOVERS SHOULD NOT REMAIN FRIENDS

▼

*Okay, I lied. Nothings perfect.*
—*Anonymous*

Okay, I know I told you this was going to be an upbeat look at the way ex-lovers can remain friends. So why am I now going to tell you when and why you shouldn't remain friends? The contradiction is illusory. A positive transition to a lasting and rewarding different friendship after breakup is not a panacea for life's difficulties. Let's face it, there are also good reasons to just cut your losses and split. Nothing is perfect.

I've placed this chapter in the middle of the book for two reasons. First, I want to be clear about the fact that I do not take lightly the possible difficulties which you may face in transitioning from lovers to friends and beyond. Second, I want you to be aware of the good reasons for either going slowly through the transition from lover to friends, or not going through it at all, at least until you learn how. Over the years I've learned that we humans are quite clever at overlooking the most obvious blocks in the way of our own growth. Until these important blocks are removed either by changes in ourselves, in the relationship, or in our partner, all the good advice in the world won't create a satisfying friendship. This caveat applies not only to ex-lover friendships but to other kinds of friendship as well.

But I don't view what I suggest in these pages as absolute rules or as a new set of repressive "shoulds." Doing so, you might impose unnecessary restrictions on your relationships and cause yourself more pain. Situations can be changed, but evaluate the relative benefit of struggling for change in your situation to determine what action you take in relation to your ex-partner.

The best way to use my advice or anyone else's is to remember that you are an individual. Studying yourself and discovering what you want and need is an important step in the change process. Self-knowledge plus sound advice is the best guide.

The following are good reasons for at least suspending your attempts to be friends with your ex. Keep them in mind as you evaluate the direction your relationship is taking, or plan the direction you wish to see it go.

1. When you have evidence that you or your ex-partner is avoiding the reality of the change in your relationship.
2. When the friendship is an unhealthy block to your personal growth and development.
3. When mental or physical abuse plays a part in the way you behave together.
4. When the relationship hinders formation of your new relationships.
5. When your repeated efforts to be friendly toward each other end up in emotionally draining disappointment.
6. When you are maintaining contact purely to save face or to sport an image.
7. When you or your partner simply do not want to be friends.

## Avoiding the Reality of Change

The reality of the loss of a couple relationship and the pain of its loss are powerful forces which both parties must face. Masking failure to accept the change in the relationship under the guise of continuing a platonic "friendship" can have powerfully destructive effects.

Elizabeth and Rex, whose story is told in more detail in chapter two, discovered each other over twenty-five years ago, and became sexually involved after several years of intense friendship. They separated after Elizabeth got pregnant. Elizabeth decided to keep the child, but to break off her relationship with Rex, believing that the baby deserved to be born but that she did not want in any way to block Rex's path to success. Unwed motherhood over twenty-five years ago was of course far more difficult and stigmatized than it is today.

Two years ago a friend pointed out to Elizabeth that while she now saw Rex and herself as friends, not the lovers they had been some twenty-five years before, she was still reserving romantic energy for him.

At this point, Elizabeth made a discovery:

*I really was not aware that I was carrying a blinding torch for him for twenty-five years. Because of this I went from one destructive relationship to another. I think I was just unconsciously leaving myself available for him. Only when I was able to drop the illusion was I able to have a real "friendship" with him and a happy romantic relationship with another man.*

One reason that Elizabeth was unable to truly break the couple relationship was that from the very beginning her account of its demise was only partially accurate. Her belief that she gave up the relationship so that Rex would be unencumbered was only part of the story. She had never really consciously acknowledged her own reasons for wanting the breakup. She left Rex in part because *she* was feeling overpowered by him. After they broke up she regularly thought first of what Rex would want her to do with her life before listening to herself. Not only was she unconsciously avoiding the reality of change, but she was avoiding taking responsibility for her needs.

Following Elizabeth's example, you would be wise to carefully scrutinize your motives for the breakup as well as for maintaining the friendship lest you get stuck, unable to move forward. Unconscious or unacknowledged motivations can elude even your most persistent and earnest self-examination. If you suspect that you have not completely accepted the reality of the change in your relationship, I suggest that you employ a qualified therapist to help you acknowledge your real motives and accept the reality of the situation.

In addition to gaining understanding of the perhaps unconscious blocks to accepting the change in your relationship, do what you can to take care of yourself during the process of separation and transition. Self-care and taking responsibility for yourself will support your ability to acknowledge the change. In chapter five, on "Taking Care of Yourself," you will learn steps you can take and tasks you will need to accomplish to adjust to the loss of parts of the relationship. In mourning a relationship, for example, some people get stuck in the "denial" stage, their minds refusing to entertain the reality of the situation as a way of defending their emotions. If this is the case for you, you may be building your new friendship on the false notion that the romance is not lost but only temporarily misplaced.

▼

## When the Friendship Is an Unhealthy Block to Your Own Growth and Development

At first blush, this question of whether the ongoing postbreakup relationship blocks your own development might seem to point to the same problem as simply not getting over the loss or avoiding the reality of change. But personal development can be subtle and take place on levels of personality, emotions, and social relationships, as well as spiritually.

Many people decided to break up their couple relationship because they felt it was doing damage to their personal development—either normal development or development related to unresolved trauma from their families of origin. Normal development includes the changes in our psychological or social situations that are part of the common process of human growth and development. These are tied to our age and our social status in our families and community. Learning to be more interdependent with our intimates, giving of ourselves to the community, having children, or taking personal time for self-exploration are examples of normal developmental experiences.

Developmental *tasks* which may be related to unresolved trauma include learning to feel basic trust toward others, learning to maintain a clear sense of the boundary between ourselves and others, and learning to develop a healthy relationship with members of the opposite sex. The same need for personal development that might cause a breakup can also serve as a reasonable basis for maintaining distance in the postbreakup relationship.

Phillip and Susan were married for ten years. During the entire period of their marriage, they struggled over Susan's extreme dependence on Phillip in numerous areas of their lives and the corresponding difficulties Phillip experienced setting limits on his giving. For several years they worked with a counselor to try to cope with Susan's intense need to be taken care of and Phillip's

▼

reciprocal inability to set limits on her demands. Even though she was well aware of the disproportionate way in which she demanded things from Phillip, Susan was unable to control her behavior. After a prolonged struggle to cope with this issue they decided to break off the relationship.

In part because Phillip and Susan had struggled so hard to keep their couple relationship together, they felt a particularly strong desire to retain some kind of friendly contact after the breakup. In therapy, they were able to set relatively clear boundaries around most of their activities. Within two years, both Phillip and Susan had new relationships and appeared to be moving in healthy directions. Susan's struggle with her intense need to be taken care of, however, was beginning to emerge in her new relationship and continued in her friendship with Phillip, despite their agreement to correct their own sides of this negative interaction that clearly blocked Susan's development. Making matters worse, now that Susan was involved with her new partner Dagmar, and had Phillip as a friend, she had little opportunity to struggle with her anxiety that her needs would be frustrated, an anxiety which commonly led her to act in a very dependent, self-diminishing way. Phillip, on the other hand, had remarried a woman quite different from Susan who was self-motivated and required little of him. Without his new partner to serve, Phillip was vulnerable to the cries for help from Susan, no matter how large or small. It is clear then that this continual "friendship" between Phillip and Susan had a consistent negative effect on their individual ability not to react to one another or play into one another's weaknesses.

Following a breakup, part of your task will be to regain your sense of self-esteem and competence. Sometimes if the friendship is established too soon the individuals will not have had enough time to regain this necessary balance. Dagmar, an organizational consultant now involved with Susan, said of a previous relationship,

> *Because the relationship was destructive to who I felt I was, it was not one of helping to build. It wasn't helping to build your egos [self-esteem] but helping to tear them down. This happens sometimes when it is a very competitive relationship.*

Development is synonymous with change. Sometimes, maintaining the friendship after the breakup may be a block to the normal changes we seek. As Joan points out, what we need at any given time can be different from what we wanted in the past:

> *I don't need another playmate right now. It would be nice for me now to have another [committed] relationship rather than continuing to build a larger group of "friends."*

This is a good example of a situation in which continuing the friendship might distract you from what you need to do for yourself. Since she has a wide network of friends, Joan doesn't want another ex-lover/friend but would rather work towards a more committed relationship where she could raise a family.

Stacks and stacks of books have been written trying to describe "healthy" personal and relationship growth. Yet the issue is still not settled. You must decide for yourself what is healthy. While I cannot decide for you whether or not the friendship you are attempting to maintain is a block in your developmental path, you might ask yourself the following questions to help yourself decide whether or not you are stuck, and, if so, whether the negative relationship is the glue.

1. How much does the opinion of your ex-partner affect your choices about what you want to think, feel, or do for and about yourself?

2. Do you find yourself daydreaming excessively about your ex-relationship when you are having difficulties in daily life?
3. Are you actively pursuing the other relationships and activities of interest to you?
4. Do you often avoid contact with other friends in the hope that you will get together with your ex-lover?
5. Are you moving through the stages of emotions which follow a breakup (see chapter five, "Taking Care of Yourself"), or are you just stuck?
6. Are you moving toward being the best you can be for yourself?

Whether your relationships with other friends, aside from your ex-partner, are healthy or growing in a "healthy" direction is also an important concern. And attaining a successful balance or emotional alignment within these other relationships will positively affect your self-esteem, and enable you to better handle your ex-lover friendship.

## When Emotional, Mental, or Physical Abuse Are Prominent in the Way You Behave Together

Much research in domestic violence and other forms of abuse suggests that partners who are seriously abusive rigorously deny that they are in fact abusive. Dishonesty alone is a good reason for not attempting to remain friends with your ex-partner, especially when he or she continues to be abusive without admitting to and then changing behavior.

Unfortunately, people who are abused often have great difficulty acknowledging that they are being abused. The next question you might ask is, "How do I know if I am being abused?" There is no simple answer. The following list of questions may help you think about whether you are being or have been physically or mentally abused in your relationship. In that these questions are only suggestive of some level of abuse, you must honestly confront the nature of your relationship and, if it is abusive, the minimal likelihood of change in the near future.

While everyone is capable of committing one or more of these abusive actions, what is important for you to assess is how often, with what provocation, and with what sense of personal responsibility are they enacted.

## Are You Being Abused? [1]

The following questions about your partner will help you gauge the frequency and level of abuse in your relationship and its effects on you. Score each of the items on the list according to the designated scale. Then go over the results with an eye on, (1) the sheer number of abusive actions, (2) the number of frequent abuses related to each item, and (3) the total level of abuse. To get this last estimate add up the scores from all of the items. Since no comparative statistics are available, you will have to make your own assessment of how much is too much.

> 1 = **never**
> 2 = **rarely**
> 3 = **occasionally**
> 4 = **frequently**
> 5 = **very frequently**

**1.** Does he/she continually monitor your time and make you account for every minute (when you run errands, visit friends, commute to work, etc.)? Score \_\_\_\_\_

**2.** Does he/she ever accuse you of having affairs with others or act suspicious that you are? Score _____

**3.** Is he/she ever rude to your friends? Score _____

**4.** Does he/she ever discourage you from starting friendships with others? Score _____

**5.** Do you ever feel isolated and alone, as if you have nobody close to you to confide in? Score _____

**6.** Is he/she overly critical of daily things, such as your cooking, your clothes, or your appearance? Score _____

**7.** Does he/she demand a strict account of how you spend money, or do you quarrel over financial matters? Score _____

**8.** Do his/her moods change radically, from very calm to very angry, or vice versa? Score _____

**9.** Is he/she disturbed by you working or by the thought of you working? Score _____

**10.** Does he/she become angry more easily when drinking? Score _____

**11.** Does he/she pressure you for sex much more often than you'd like? Score _____

**12.** Does he/she become angry if you don't want to go along with his/her requests for sex? Score _____

**13.** Do you quarrel much about having children or raising them? Score _____

**14.** Does he/she ever strike you with his/her hands or feet (slap, punch, kick, etc.)? Score _____

**15.** Does he/she ever threaten or strike you with an object or weapon? Score _____

**16.** Has he/she ever threatened to kill either him- or herself or you? Score _____

**17.** Is he/she ever violent toward children? Score _____

**18.** Is he/she ever violent toward other people outside your home and family? Score _____

**19.** Does he/she ever throw objects or break things when angry? Score _____

As some of the questions in this list suggest, emotional abuse is just as much a part of abuse as physical abuse. The problem, of course, is getting clear about what we really mean by emotional abuse. Showing you an example of emotional abuse is easier than attempting to define it.

Randa and Roy met two years ago in a bar. Even though Roy is twenty-eight years old, she is Roy's first serious relationship. Randa has been involved in a series of destructive relationships. In her words, "I always end up with guys that take advantage of me and abuse me." But she can't understand why.

Randa, a twenty-nine-year-old dental assistant, lives in an apartment that, without her mother's knowledge, was paid for by her father. Since the age of twelve, Randa has been battling often overwhelming feelings that her parents hate her and are looking for some way to get rid of her. She is still so attached to her father that she cannot go a week without somehow getting him to intervene in her life, but she resents him for doing so.

Roy, a technician, lives with his parents. He works sporadically during the day as a refrigerator technician and spends his free time drinking beer and hanging out at bars with his male friends. Like Randa, Roy is constantly at war with his parents, but seems completely unable to separate himself from them or their protection. Both Roy and Randa mentioned that Roy and his friends often speak very disparagingly of women in general and have been rude to the extreme with Randa. It is obvious to even the most casual observer that they continue to be snared by potent and destructive dynamics left over from their families of origin, and that neither has made much progress towards becoming emotional adults.

Despite their extreme, blind passion for each other, the cycle of emotional abuse between Roy and Randa has gone unchanged since they met. A few examples of the abusive interactions will give you the picture.

On the third night after they met, Randa told Roy that if he really loved her he would stop going out with his friends and spend most of his time with her. Roy pulled over to the side of the road and forced Randa to walk five miles back to her home.

Two weeks after Roy and Randa met, Roy asked Randa to move into his parents' house with him; one week later she moved in. One night Roy found Randa eating ice cream when he came home from the bar. When he discovered that it was his favorite kind of ice cream and she had finished what was left, Roy flew into a rage. He forbade her to *ever* eat ice cream in *his* house again if he was not present. Shattered and confused, Randa said little and went to bed early. The next night at the bar he ridiculed Randa in front of his peers, saying that she was fat because she had eaten his ice cream.

The day after that, Randa told Roy that she hated him and never wanted to see him again. But since she had no place to go she did not follow through with her threat.

A few nights later, Roy and Randa were at home talking about how much they loved each other and about the possibility of marriage. The next day Roy reported to Randa that he would be leaving the following week for the army and didn't know if he really wanted to see her again. Randa broke all of his favorite record albums.

At this point Randa and Roy broke up for the sixth time. Two weeks later, in our conversation, Randa said, "My therapist thinks I should stay away from Roy. But he's my buddy. We're really good friends. We don't have a commitment while he's in the service so we're just friends. But I just can't get the love for him out of my mind." Asked what she thought Roy was feeling at this point, she replied, "I don't know. He hasn't returned my calls or answered my daily letters. He's probably just busy."

Randa and Roy's behavior and Randa's obvious state of denial regarding the actual state of their relationship indicate that the abusive cycle they engaged in as a couple is unlikely to change in the postbreakup relationship. They are both snared by potent and destructive family dynamics, and neither has made progress towards becoming emotional adults. In fact, it is likely that they will each continue to reenact this dynamic in future relationships until they resolve the issues which continue with their original families. For them, there will be little to gain by attempting to maintain a "friendship" at this time.

Oliver, a forty-year-old attorney, pointed to another kind of abuse which might be a good reason for not maintaining a friendship:

*There was just something about the way we were together. We always seemed to bring the worst out in each other. If I was trying to build my life anew she would always offer me drugs and down we went. We fit together like the hands of a man in a coffin.*

This kind of mutual, collusive abuse is sometimes difficult to spot and stop since you each tend to validate the other's negative behavior. If one partner attempts to change towards being less self-destructive, the relationship is upset. Basic unsettled psychological needs in ourselves can be at the root of intensely passionate and, at the same time, terribly destructive relationships. If you feel that your sense of well being and self-esteem is continually low or under attack your best bet is to withdraw from the relationship until you feel more satisfied with your right to feel good about yourself.

## When the Formation of Your New Relationship Is Hindered

Again Joan's comments from the perspective of concentrating on building a committed relationship are useful.

*I don't need another playmate right now. It would be nice for me now to have another [committed] relationship rather than continuing to build a larger group of "friends." It wouldn't be the best for who I am at this point in time.*

To begin and to foster new intimate relationships in the early part of the transition process of your previous couple relationship can be complex and stressful. This is in part because "coupling" generally requires a period when the pair cordon themselves off from the world emotionally, psychologically, and even physically to build the foundation for their future together. During this period, outside involvement with an ex-partner often produces premature questioning by the new partner about the security of the new relationship. In self-defense he or she may withhold deepening commitment.

If this is the case, perhaps the process of creating the post-breakup friendship with your ex-partner is best put on hold until the new relationship is more solid. But this consideration depends greatly upon the personality of the individuals involved and the nature of the new relationship. The new couple should openly discuss the issue. In the section on what couples can do for each other, in chapter six, I will offer other ways to handle this situation.

## Maintaining an Image

If your reason for maintaining a friendship with your ex is for "keeping up an image," beware! Closely evaluate yourself. Retaining an image may not be utterly meaningless, but it may be an unnecessary burden on you during an already difficult time.

Several decades ago couples often elected to stay together even after facing the truth of their disenchantment simply to maintain a socially respectable image, or because they thought they would thus avoid hurting their children, family, and friends. Nowadays the needs and concerns of children, extended family, and friends are less important in a couple's decision whether or not to separate. This attitude does not reflect their heartlessness, but rather that they feel that everyone would benefit from the change, including themselves. Indeed research has found that relationships between children and their individual parents, particularly their fathers, have improved after the separation.[2] Reports from adult children of divorced parents indicate that, in retrospect, they believe their lives might have been better if their parents had divorced earlier rather than continue to live together in obvious pain and resentment.

So when you are thinking about your relationship, be certain that you are clear that the friendship is what you *want* and that you are not persisting in it mainly for the purpose of maintaining or protecting an image for others.

## You or Your Ex-Partner Just Don't Wanna

Perhaps the most common and seemingly obvious reason mentioned by the study participants for not attempting to maintain a friendship with an ex-lover was that "he [she] just didn't want to be friends anymore." The reasons that people do not want to be friends are no doubt unique to their situation and may or may not change as times passes. The process of transitioning from lovers to friends can be long and arduous, so it is important to remember that time may reveal an interest in friendship which does not exist immediately following the breakup. Forcing your ex-partner to move too quickly may ultimately push him or her away. And you may go through a phase of wanting nothing from your ex in the way of communication or sharing.

## Some Not-So-Right Reasons for Abandoning the Relationship

In contrast to these more valid reasons for not continuing the relationship after breakup, there are several reasons I have heard which make little or no sense.

1. Feeling guilty or dumb for remaining friends.
2. Concern about protecting other friends and family.
3. Unrealistic blaming of your partner for the breakup.
4. That without children there is no need to be friends.

### Feeling Guilty or Dumb for Remaining Friends

I was amazed to discover how many of the people responding to my advertisement for participants in the study told me that they appreciated the fact that I was conducting this research because for once they felt okay about having their friendships. Jackie, in discussing the reactions of others, said:

*I really appreciated the help that I got from both the other participants and the staff in the divorce workshops. But I often felt confused and angry because each time I indicated that I was trying to work out a real friendship and not just a business relationship with my ex-husband they called me stupid and said things like, "Why do you want to be friends with that S.O.B. anyway?" They just didn't seem to understand that this could be a good thing for both of us and our children as well.*

Often others around you will simply fail to appreciate the value of your continued relatedness. They have fallen prey to many myths and outdated views about changing relationships and just do not know any better. Remember, too, that family members and friends each have their own private interest in the nature of your relationship.

## Concern about Protecting Other Friends and Family

Your transition from lovers to friends may be as difficult for your other friends and family as it is for you. If they have been friends with you and your ex-partner together, not only will they be feeling the loss of your relationship and of this way of relating to you, but they will also be confused at times as to how they are to behave with each of you. Their divided loyalty to you and your ex-partner may leave them worried about how each of you is feeling at the same time. You may experience their anxiety as a statement against your continuing friendship with your ex-partner. This may or may not be the case. At this junction it is important to communicate openly with them and enlist their support.

Another difficult scenario is when your friends and family prefer to keep their relationship with you but not your ex-partner. In this case you may be tempted to join them in their rejection of and anger toward your ex-partner to make things easier on them. If you take this tack they will be relieved of the problem of spending time with someone they dislike. But at what cost to you? As you read in chapter two, many people have recently discovered a wide array of benefits in remaining friends which you might miss if you choose this rejecting approach prematurely.

## Unrealistic Blaming of Your Partner for the Breakup

If you continue to blame the other and failure to take stock of your own responsibility for not only the negative but for the positive aspects of your relationship, you will have yet another unnecessary reason to not transform your relationship into friendship.

## Without Children There's No Need to Be Friends

A primary reason many people give for attempting to work out a positive, not simply businesslike, relationship is for the sake of the children. Conversely, however, I have frequently heard people say "if there are no children involved, there is no reason to maintain the relationship."

In response to this attitude I can only suggest that you weigh this wholesale dismissal of the value of a continued, albeit transformed, relationship against the benefits of maintaining friendship that so many people have reported. Weigh the benefits of maintaining a friendship with your lost lover as they apply to your own situation whether or not children are involved.

CHAPTER

# 5

# TAKING CARE OF YOURSELF—
# FOR THE RELATIONSHIP

▼

This chapter is about what you must do to rebuild and take care of yourself after the breakup. The survival and growth of the individual is a formidable and necessary part of the transition process. Some of the many useful books available on what the *individual* must accomplish to survive and to find growth opportunity in divorce or breakup are listed at the back of this book. Taking care of yourself is very important both for yourself and in the interest of laying the foundation for friendship with your ex-partner. Your separate coping efforts will be crucial to maintaining the kind of valuable friendship that can have great personal meaning.

All of the participants that I interviewed for this book pointed out that the successful transition from lovers to friends depends greatly upon each person's success coping with the transition as an individual as well as a member of an uncoupling pair.

## Rubbing Your Stomach and Patting Your Head at the Same Time

The transition from lovers to friends is similar to other life transitions such as changing jobs, graduating, becoming parents, experiencing personal loss, and aging. Much more is being written each day about these transitions and how to cope with them.

Life transitions such as losing a job, graduating from college, or facing the death of a friend require that we courageously work our way through stages of transition (including the stages of loss) and ultimately turn our affections and efforts in some new and rewarding direction as individuals.

In his widely read book *Making Sense of Life's Changes*, William Bridges describes three natural stages of transition processes in general: *endings*, passing through the *neutral zone*, and making *new beginnings*. Endings are essential steps in the process of change which make up a large part of living. Since each of us has a history of coping with endings (of jobs, loves, projects, etc.), Bridges suggests that we survey our own private ways of coping with endings, but that we also recognize common aspects of the natural ending experience: disengagement, disidentification, disenchantment, and disorientation.

The *neutral zone* is the period during which Dr. Bridges suggests we take the time to reevaluate our life hopes and aspirations, our "real wantings," as a way of setting the stage for a successful new beginning.

*New beginnings*, then, arise out of the reorientation of the neutral zone, bringing together what we want and the real world of actual opportunity. As I will explain, making the transition from lovers to friends is significantly different from other transitions. Nevertheless, I encourage you to read this excellent book to further assist you.[1]

The transition from lovers to friends is different from the others because the process of change takes place at multiple levels and goes in two different directions. Working on personal changes while working on your positive transition from lovers to friends is a juggling act that can be both difficult and rewarding. Most of my interviewees mentioned that they needed at least some period of time separated from their ex-partner, from two days to ten years, to work through the changes and losses of the many aspects of the couple relationship before they were ready to even act "as if" they were friends.

Changing from lovers to friends is like changing jobs, moving to a new community, and becoming a family but it is also quite different. At the emotional and psychological levels a similar situation is that of a mother giving birth extremely prematurely. At the time that she is still in love with her *dream* of the child to be, she must prepare for the possible death of that child. Then she must readjust to a newborn who may be quite different from her prior expectations, and finally she must come to accept the limitations of her new relationship with the child, adjusting her behavior and feelings to the emerging behavior of the child. If she is successful, the loving essence of this relationship will flourish.

The movement from the ending phase to the neutral zone and onto the new beginning is particularly difficult in the transition from lovers to friends because you must *simultaneously*

1. reject what you don't want from the couple relationship in the postbreakup friendship;
2. face and accept the loss of that which you want but can't have;
3. evaluate and support those elements of the relationship that will form the foundation for the new friendship;
4. make a new beginning on your own separate future.

And in that you will be transitioning within a relationship rather than from it, you must to some extent negotiate the enactment of each of these tasks with your ex-partner. This necessity of negotiation in the transition adds a significant challenge to the process. Since a failure to negotiate precipitates the downfall of many couple relationships, the need to negotiate a new kind of relationship with your ex-partner is a bit like rubbing your stomach and patting your head at the same time.

Most of the people I have interviewed who have successfully made the positive transition from lovers to friends mentioned that they were able to accomplish these tasks only to varying degrees and at different times during the transition process.

One way to manage this problem of struggling with opposing feelings is by using what I call the Horoscope Technique.

**The Horoscope Technique.** One reason you may get stuck in the obsessive knot of angry or resentful feelings, to the exclusion of your more positive ones, is that you may be concerned about "losing" the angry feelings and being seduced by your ex-partner into acknowledging *only* the positive feelings. While it's possible to have many different and even contradictory feelings towards your ex-partner, it is very difficult to experience them consciously at the same time. Knowing this, you can allow yourself to go with one feeling at one moment and return to the others later. The goal is to let go of one contradictory feeling in order to experience the other. The purpose of experiencing the feelings in the first place is so that you can either enjoy them or work them through to a more positive resolution.

## The Technique

Sit down and write yourself a note that reads like a horoscope prediction. First, write something very favorable which indicates good fortune for yourself. For example, "You will soon see new ways to conquer your financial dreams." Next write the following: "For today, do not allow your feeling of _____ to disrupt your chance to experience the deeper feelings of compassion and friendship between you and someone you care about."

The advantages of this technique are that it reassures you that you will not "forget" your negative feelings; it structures your interaction with your ex-partner by allowing you to communicate singular aspects of your experience; and it validates both contradictory feelings which in essence validates *you!*

## Hints for Taking Care of Yourself for the Friendship

As a result of both the complexity and difficulty of the process of breaking up, the potential for both deep suffering and profound growth are great. At a minimum, in order to recover from the breakup and prepare yourself for a successful transition to lasting friendship, you must:

1. Build a firm foundation of high self-esteem.
2. Learn the art of gaining perspective.
3. Accept that there are things that you can't control.
4. Accept the end of the old relationship and embrace the new.
5. Take responsibility for your share in the breakdown of the relationship.
6. Move beyond the myths of simple ambivalence about the breakup and your ex-partner.
7. Look for the negative aspects of your ex-partner's behavior—but with caution and only as long as necessary to gain emotional distance.
8. Create a new and improved sense of personal identity.

9. Emotionally realign yourself with other aspects of your life outside of intimate relationships and find alternative sources for meeting your interpersonal needs.
10. Don't merely function. Be creative; freely choose what you want for yourself and your relationship.

## Build Your Foundation of Resilient Self-Esteem

The importance of self-esteem as the foundation for resolving any of life's difficulties can not be overestimated. It is so important that in 1986, the state of California enacted a law establishing a special California Task Force to Promote Self-esteem and Personal and Social Responsibility. The recently published task force report, *Toward a State of Self-esteem*, is a tremendous service to people. The task force officially defined self-esteem as "Appreciating my own worth and importance and having the character to be accountable for myself and to act responsibly toward others."[2] Unfortunately, we don't always recognize the value of self-esteem in our repertoire of abilities because we confuse selfishness and self-esteem. Recognize, however, that an essential aspect of good self-esteem is the "appreciation of the worth of others and the importance of acting responsibly towards them." Caring for others enhances your self-esteem.

Building self-esteem works wonders as the foundation for making a positive transition from lovers to friends. When you are aware of and accept your own worth you are more able to give yourself and your ex-partner permission to act in new ways. You become aware of the degree to which you can control your own destiny and control the present moment. Freedom to act positively emerges from the combination of self- and other-acceptance: a key ingredient in maintaining self-esteem.

With a strong sense of self-esteem you have the emotional strength to accept yourself as a whole person capable of both failures and success in living, including the successes and the problems which characterized your relationship with your ex-partner. This stance facilitates a positive transition.

In his book, *How to Raise Your Self-Esteem*, Nathaniel Branden points out that only when you are able to accept yourself can you be truly aware of who you are as a person. Without this knowledge you will not be able to be aware of the choices available to you. With it options come alive. You'll find annotated references to this and other books on building and maintaining self-esteem in the bibliography.

Three things I recommend you do to build self-esteem for yourself and for the relationship are first, acknowledge those things you like *and* dislike about yourself, second, accept that these are all parts of you, and third, seek out ways to appreciate others around you. It is not necessary for you to like everything you notice about yourself. But change can only occur once we acknowledge what is—only awareness leads to the opportunity to choose.

Affirming on a daily basis that you are a person of worth and importance can serve not only to build your self-esteem but also guide you in creating an image of the person that you want to be. You can affirm yourself in several ways. First, write a list of those ways in which you appreciate yourself as a whole person, for example as parent, friend, lover, Mr. Fixit, a person who cares, etc. If you have difficulty arriving at things you appreciate about yourself, this is the time to use your trusted friends: ask them to tell you about your strengths. Add their suggestions to the list. At least once a day, preferably in the morning, say to yourself, "These are the many ways in which I appreciate myself..." and now read the list of items that you have constructed.[3]

A variation of this exercise is to develop the habit of spending some time each evening reflecting on your day. Write down what you liked about yourself that day. Do not be discouraged by the difficulty you might have in thinking about ways in which you appreciate yourself. I am always amazed at how much easier it is for people to point out the things they dislike about themselves than it is for them to acknowledge what they like.

The third method for building your self-esteem is to seek out ways in which you can express your appreciation of the worth and value of other people around you. To the degree you can handle it emotionally, you can specifically look for ways in which you can express your appreciation for your ex-partner. Of course, you will need to monitor the effect of making positive statements about your ex-partner to insure that you are not making the separation process more difficult for yourself. As a first step in this other-focused approach to building self-esteem, write down what strikes you as positive in the way you both have handled the breakup. If you have each made kind gestures towards each other at any time place each of these on your list. Before you meet with your ex-partner review this list and acknowledge your appreciation to yourself or him or her.

## Learn the Art of Gaining Perspective
Because we have some degree of free will in our lives, each action we take is promoted or restrained by the point of view or perspective which guides us. For example, by clutching tightly to a benevolent perspective it is possible for a mother to say to the child who has just spread indelible ink on her favorite evening gown, "I love you but I am very angry that you spread ink on my gown. Next time I want you to be more careful." Not only can she say these words but she feels what she says. Unfortunately due to the inevitable collision of thoughts and feelings of breaking up, a personal perspective that enables us instead of disabling us often gets lost in the struggle to get through the pain.

In my work in individual therapy with clients, we use several methods to help the client quickly gain an enabling perspective in what often seem to be intractable situations. These include *taking a helicopter view* of the situation and *reframing* what is before you.

**Take the Helicopter View.** Imagine that you are viewing the "action" of a specific incident, or your relationship as a whole from the bubble of a helicopter high above the scene. As you gain altitude take advantage of the fact that helicopters are frequently quite noisy. Imagine that you can selectively hear or screen out the angry or at times thoughtlessly hurtful statements each of you is making. Imagine that you must inject into the conversation the words you would like to be saying and hearing. That is, because there is ambiguity in what you might be hearing you can improve the likelihood of a positive outcome by knowingly choosing to inject the words that, for you, would make the outcome better.

Another advantage of hovering high above the situation in your helicopter is that you can see for some distance. You can see out into the future of your relationship. You can make use of this vantage point to see beyond, into the future and to construct a mental image of the way you want things to be.

The view from above can also be used in conjunction with other efforts you must make to take care of yourself for the relationship, such as looking to the past to discover your role in the changes you are facing.

**Use Reframing.** Another way of gaining a new perspective is to reframe what you perceive in the action between your partner and yourself. Reframing a situation or behavior essentially redefines the meaning of the situation or behavior for some purpose.[4] You create an interpretation or understanding of actions and motives, based on a fundamental belief that people are doing the best that they can do at the time. Reframed, their behavior not only makes sense but can be seen as directed towards solving, rather than creating, a problem.

For example, a child was dragged into my office several years ago because his parents were enraged that he would not go to school. They believed that he was not going to school because "he's just lazy and doesn't want to face the music for failing to finish his homework." After some discussion, I discovered that when Johnny didn't go to school, his parents were much less likely to fight, as they had increasingly done over the preceding months. With this in mind I reframed Johnny's behavior by pointing out to Johnny and his parents that even though he was only six years old Johnny knew much about love. Further, he felt that it was his duty to stay at home to prevent his parents from fighting. I am not certain that this was the "real" reason that Johnny resisted going to school. What was important was that the meaning of his behavior be reframed to serve our work on the struggle between the parents. It turned out that Johnny resisted going to school only once after the reframing session, once the parents began to work on their problems. I had little evidence that my interpretation of Johnny's behavior was correct. But the strategy I chose to adopt worked, making the point that helpful fiction can be as useful as validation of fact in bringing about positive change.

There are two ways you can use the technique of reframing to gain an enabling perspective on your and your ex-partner's behavior. First, you can understand your actions as rational, caring ways of solving problems between or within each of you. If, for example, your ex-partner hangs up the telephone in the middle of a heated discussion, rather than escalating into a rage, perceiving the action as insulting and controlling, you might try to perceive his or her actions as an effort to protect what feelings of respect and caring might exist between you. He or she might have been trying to avoid saying hurtful things that would have made regaining each other's trust more difficult at a later time.

A second way of using reframing is as a space holder as you seek meaning in the stream of confusing, angry, saddening events during the breakup. This way, simply as a matter of economics, you will have fewer negative or destructive meanings with which to contend.

## Work Through Loss to Acceptance

Much has been written about the importance of working as an individual through the stages of loss when coming to terms with the loss of a significant relationship. But working through the experience of loss of the "couple" part of your relationship can be even more difficult when you are attempting to remain friends at the same time. You might experience shock, anger, resentment, and sadness at the loss of some parts of the relationship, while at the same time or in sequence appreciating the continuation or even enhancement of other parts. For example, you will need to face the loss of extended time together but at the same time embrace your new freedom to talk about issues that were taboo when you were a couple.

The number of dissolutionment trajectories, or forms of transition, are perhaps as many as the couples that experience them. And each partner's specific constellation of feelings at any given time will be different too. For example, if at the time of the breakup both of you feel little desire to remain friends, perhaps out of anger or resentment, you will cope with the loss of your coupleness in a very different way than if one or both of you hope for a friendly postbreakup relationship.

If you already envision and hope for friendship at the time

that you are deciding to break up, the transition process will include some seemingly contradictory and conflicting experiences. You will need to move toward accepting the loss of aspects of coupleness, while holding in proper perspective the memory traces and arcs of coupleness which will always exist. You will also need to embrace and maintain those aspects of the friendship such as intimate communication, intellectual sharing, sexual contact, acknowledgment of the specialness of shared history, which you wish to maintain. If you are not ready to try to be friends but choose to stay out of contact, the contradictions and conflicts may be less apparent at any given time.

Although you will retain some intimacy if friendship prevails after a breakup, you will still need to confront your undesired loss of certain aspects of your prior coupleness. You will likely confront the feelings of shock, anger, resentment, sadness, and ultimately acceptance, which often accompany any loss, particularly that of a significant person. In therapy with my clients, confronting their acceptance of loss is often remarkably difficult, in part because clients feel guilty for successfully letting go of the relationship.

What do I mean when I say that you will lose aspects of coupleness at the transition? The people I interviewed felt that they lost time together, the guiding image of coupleness, relationships with family and friends, someone to talk to with instant understanding of complex feelings and situations, safety from the feeling of being alone, and important parts of their future dream. Most people said that they missed time together doing various small things. Your list will be different, and specific to your own situation.

The loss of the image of partnership is a particular one. When you were together it seemed to be there automatically. Toward the end of your relationship, however, the effort to maintain it may have been more deliberate and more of a challenge, more of a strain.

I was surprised by the number of people—nearly half of those I interviewed—who said that they would have greatly missed their in-laws if they had not remained friends after the breakup. Many said that they were surprised at their intense feelings of loss for mothers-, fathers-, sisters-, and brothers-in-law.

After living together or spending a great deal of time together, couples develop significant knowledge about each other. With this come a certain ease of expression and an experience of intellectual, emotional, and spiritual similarity, and a diminished feeling of aloneness. Whether the similarity is real or not often seems to be of little consequence. Losing this feeling of connectedness can be both painful and disorienting.

It is often only after some probing that my clients discover how important their ex-partners were as stabilizing, guiding factors in their vision of their own future. They then frequently remark that they often felt lost trying to imagine a future without the sense of coupleness they once had with their partners.

## Coping with the Feeling of Being Out of Control in the "Land of Chaos"

It is profoundly important to the future of your friendship that you cope with the sense of being out of control. When you feel out of control, you are more likely to say or do things that you won't be able to take back. The sense of being out of control can include an actual bodily sense of being cramped, difficulty breathing, uncontrollable tearfulness, fear, impulses to try to salvage the relationship at whatever the cost, and sometimes blinding rage. A patient of mine once told me:

*It doesn't seem to matter what I do. I wander around the house staring at the walls. She comes into the room. We try to discuss our feelings and it always ends in anger, disappointment, and confusion. Then it comes over me: my stomach begins to twist, I feel like I can't breathe, none of what I know I should do to take care of myself works. I feel so lost. I can't breathe. I can't think.*

At these times great advice often goes right out the window. But try to remember the following six approaches, which are especially helpful for regaining some modest sense of balance and control:

1. Recognize that the intense feelings come not only from your adult mind, but from your "inner child."
2. Have a visual and verbal image of the emotional, psychological, and spiritual person you want to be after the breakup.
3. Set limits on the interactions you have with your ex-partner.
4. Use the Reverse Spiral Technique on page 119.
5. Use your friends in a deliberate way to help you regain your sense of balance.
6. Try to convince your ex-partner *one more time* that your beliefs and needs are more right than his or hers.

**Recognize the Power of Your Inner Child.** When I asked my client Stan to tell me how old he felt when he began to fall into what he called The Land of Chaos, he replied without hesitation, "I can see myself at about five years old. I am crying and I just can't stop. I'm scared that no one will help me. My stomach is on fire. It's like the feelings I have now are that kid's feelings." When you begin to feel the Chaos attack it can be helpful to remember that it is not the competent adult that you are today who is feeling overwhelmed, but rather the small, helpless remnant of a child that resides within you. Remembering this, you can also recognize that, as an adult, you are not helpless and alone. You can discover ways to regain balance and self-worth that will lead you to surviving these moments. Recognize that your adult mind and feelings of today can help you out of this difficult situation. While the feelings of that "inner child" are important and valid, they can contribute to your sense of feeling out of control and helpless.

Aside from simply acknowledging the existence of these childlike feelings, you can use them to understand the underlying feelings which guide your behavior in all of your relationships. For example, my client said it helped him to know that his underlying feeling of despair and the thought "no one will help me" were traceable to a specific event in his life as a child. Without completely losing it, he was able to recognize that his belief was outdated. From this awareness he also eventually recognized that his decision as a child to "never count on anyone" could be released; he could trust himself as well as others to a much greater extent.

**Use Your Image of the Person You Want to Be to Bring You Through.** The days, weeks, and months following the breakup are usually not a total emotional disaster. In those moments when you're feeling a bit more rested and in control it is helpful to develop an image of the future for yourself. Keep it to draw upon when the Chaos attacks.

The technique is a simple version of visualization techniques.

Find a quiet place to relax, preferably a place that is not too familiar. Close your eyes, take several deep breaths, and feel yourself begin to relax. With your eyes still closed, imagine yourself as you might be five, ten, or fifteen years from now. Find an image that represents yourself as you will be after you successfully navigate the stormy waters of the breakup. Take your time.

Start by imagining the way you hope to look physically: the way you will be dressed, your hairstyle, and the expression on your face. Next imagine how you will feel emotionally. Finally, see yourself as a person in relation to the rest of the universe, your spiritual self. As you concentrate on this positive, comfortable image of yourself, say, "I like who I will become. I know that I will be okay."

The next time you find yourself in the Land of Chaos, excuse yourself from life for a brief period and repeat the exercise. After you say that you will be okay, imagine how you might respond either to your ex-partner or to any other aspect of your situation that leaves you feeling out of control.

**Set Limits on Interactions with Your Ex-Partner.** Says Ronald, a twenty-five-year-old nurse,
*When we began to talk about anything of any importance to either of us, no matter how rational each of our arguments seemed to each of us, the conversation just seemed to fall apart. Within minutes we were yelling at each other, she was screaming and sobbing; I was angry but felt frozen. I couldn't breathe.*

Even the best of intentions can succumb to the Chaos that emerges when partners make their last ditch effort to solve the problems that plague them. As Jan so eloquently described, the rational arguments that seem to be what are being discussed quickly get lost in the morass of hurtful feelings which overpower the best of efforts.

Both your individual growth and the future of the friendship can best be served by each person making an effort both to recognize ways in which you relate to each other that lead you to feel out of control, and to learn actions you can take to stop the destructive plunge into chaos.

Bill, for example, mentioned that whenever his partner began to accuse him of not including her in the family decision making he would feel himself getting hot all over and his breathing becoming labored. On my suggestion, Bill attempted to set useful limits in future similar circumstances by saying to his ex-partner, "I want to act in a caring way but I am frankly overwhelmed and need time to retreat and pull myself together." He was instructed to add, "and I will try to talk with you tomorrow." By using these exact words, Bill was able to set a limit on the conversation that would leave him protected but at the same time leave the relationship potentially available and undamaged.

Nothing is more useful than the obvious when all is unclear. If only we could grasp it! Perhaps the most obvious action you can take when overwhelmed by the escalating emotions of you and your partner is to agree upon and set limits about what you will confront at a given time. Vivian put her finger on this problem when she said,

*When I get so upset and out of control I want to just stop talking about the things that hurt, or just get away. But I'm scared that he will think that I am hiding or blaming him. Then everything feels even worse.*

To set useful limits on your conversations and interactions and at the same time avoid stressing yourself or the relationship even further, use these important rules.

1. Verbalize directly (not just by your behavior) that you need to withdraw.
2. Express whatever awareness you have (however great or small) of your ex-partner and his or her concerns.
3. Set a specific time at which you are willing to return to the discussion.

Verbalizing the fact that you are going to withdraw from the interaction prevents your ex-partner from having to fill in the blanks or read your mind. If he or she is forced to fill in the blanks in times of stress, his or her negative interpretation of your behavior is most likely to prevail. You might say, for example, "I know that what we are fighting about is important, but right now I am feeling overwhelmed and I need to withdraw to take care of myself." Assuming that your ex-partner is willing to take what you have said at face value he or she will not need to assume that you are blaming him or her for your feelings.

Expressing your awareness of your ex-partner's concerns is an important way of validating the other's personal worth. If you allow your partner to feel validated as a worthwhile person, you increase the likelihood that he or she will return the sentiment.

Assuming that you will want to talk about your differences when you are in better control, perhaps in the future, it will also be important to say, "Even though I am pulling away now to take care of myself, I want to talk with you again tomorrow" (or whenever you feel it might be most possible that you would be ready to talk). With such a statement you not only reassure your ex-partner that you will return, but announce that you take the issues seriously as well.

This kind of limit setting not only keeps the immediate interaction in control, but will also be important for communicating on many aspects of your evolving, sometimes jaggedly pitching and tossing relationship. Think about what limits you need and how to set them in relation to time together, types of activities, physical contact, and topics of discussion.

**The Reverse Spiral Technique.**[5] This easy-to-use technique helps you alter intense emotions that make you feel out of control. The thrust of the technique is to release you from awareness rather than make you more aware of your intense emotion. As it decreases bodily sensation associated with the negative feeling, it in turn decreases your awareness of the feeling which brought the sensations. Do the following:

**1.** Locate the spot in your body where you most intensely feel the emotion that concerns you—the bodily sensation of anger, resentment, fear, etc.

**2.** Imagine that from the center of the bodily sensation of the feeling (perhaps an ache in the stomach or tightness in the neck) a spiral is emerging.

**3.** Identify the direction in which the spiral is moving: either clockwise or counterclockwise.

**4.** Now, without trying to stop yourself from experiencing the feeling that is bothering you, imagine that the spiral is turning in the *opposite* direction. Keep your mind focused upon the spiral turning in the *opposite* direction from the way it moved when you were distressed.

**5.** After a few minutes you will feel different and note a change in your physical symptoms.

**Use Your Friends in a Deliberate, Careful Way to Help Maintain a Sense of Balance.** For some individuals, it is perhaps the most natural act to seek the support of friends and family in times of crisis. For others the most natural response is to withdraw. Friends can indeed be a valuable source of support when you are being attacked by the Chaos. Nevertheless, to balance your need for support with your desire to maintain friendship with your ex-partner, it is important to use your other friends' support in a planned, careful way.

First of all, you will need to remind them that while you want their support and guidance you *do not* want them to disparage your ex-partner. That is, while it might feel good in the short run to have a friend remind you of what an awful person your ex-partner is, the unfortunate fact is that you will remember these remarks after you recover. When you remember such remarks you might feel resentment towards your friend for saying unfair things about your lover-turned-friend.

Another negative effect of attacks by your friends on your ex-partner is that they will tend to make you focus on your ex's weaknesses rather than on your own feelings, your share of the responsibility for the breakup, or both. If you notice that your friends are using this "he or she's a rat" approach to making you feel better, you might want to say, "I know that you are trying to make me feel better by saying bad things about my ex, but this is not really helpful for me. What I want from you is for you to listen and remind me that life will get better."

**Try *One More Time* to Convince Your Ex-Partner That Your Beliefs and Needs Are More Right Than His or Hers.** When we begin to feel that we are headed for the Land of Chaos, trying to convince our partner or ex-partner that "If only you would believe that I am right" is a common strategy to attempt to regain control. If you have considered the approaches that I have described above and continue to feel that I have simply not understood the complexity or uniqueness of your situation, I suggest that you try one more time to convince your ex-partner that

▼

doing it your way will make things right. Then begin reading this section again from the beginning.

## Take Responsibility for Your Share of What Made the Relationship Untenable

Taking care to discover your role in the demise of your relationship is helpful for both you and for the future friendship. And by doing so, you can use it to make your next intimate relationship better.

As the earlier discussion of self-esteem explained, accepting yourself for who you are and taking responsibility for your thoughts and actions also contribute to your ability to be conscious of the present. If you are more aware of yourself at the moment you will be in a much better position to understand and accept the complex circumstances that led to the breakup, including your role in it. With this more reality-based understanding you will be much more available to envision the future relationship you want and work towards it.

Accepting your own responsibility for your specific contribution to the breakup allows you to know what you are *not* responsible for. If you were the person who initiated the breakup you may be feeling overly guilty and confused. These feelings may make it difficult for you to regain your self-esteem and move forward to make yourself available as a friend. Clarifying your responsibility will most likely relieve you of some of your debilitating feelings. If you were not the one to initiate the breakup, you may be feeling excessively blamed. For you, too, then it is important to know what you did and did not contribute to the breakup.

**Taking Back Your Projections.** You can work on accepting your role in the breakup by beginning to reown or take back

▼

those negative aspects of your partner's behavior which you have projected onto him/her. As a quick approach to becoming more aware of your projections try this exercise.

**1.** Bring to your consciousness your ex-partner's faults for which you blame him or her.

**2.** With the fault in mind, imagine that you are literally taking one step to the left.

**3.** As you step to the left imagine that you can visualize some of your own behavior, feelings, or thoughts just behind your partner's fault.

For example, if your ex-partner is being maddeningly controlling in a given situation, imagine him or her being bossy and controlling; imagine yourself taking one step to the left; as you imagine looking behind the ex-partner's controlling behavior you see your fear that you will go out of control with sadness.

If you are able to locate such a projected feeling, your task is to strive, first of all, to accept that you feel this way. If you are unable to cope with this feeling or thought you may want to make judicious use of your other friends or a therapist to assist you in working the feeling through. The goal of the working-through process is, in part, to regain your self-esteem by owning your full self. If you are successful, you will not only feel better for yourself but the relationship will benefit as well.

## Blaming and Name Calling: Its Use and Abuse
There may be a certain value in dwelling on and acknowledging the negative qualities of your ex-partner in the early stages of the separation process.

Diane Vaughn, in her book *Uncoupling: Turning Points in Intimate Relationships*, pointed out that for many people negative def-

▼

initions of their ex-partners are useful to a point. "When people are really uncoupled—established in a life confirming their independent identity—they will again be free to see both the positive and negative aspects of the relationship. Negative definitions are essential to the transition but they are often temporary," Vaughn writes.[6] The word *essential* may be a bit strong but my experience suggests that the point is well taken.

Looking for the negative aspects of your partner's behavior can be helpful because it helps you to establish a line or boundary between yourself and your ex-partner. In her dissertation's discussion about the relationship between affect and postdivorce well-being, Carol Masheter remarks, "No doubt, some postdivorce friendships are problematic, whereas others are beneficial. Similarly, learning to stand up to an abusive ex-spouse may require healthy hostility, otherwise hostility can be corrosive to both personal well-being and relationships."[7]

In times when you are feeling exceptionally needy some blaming can counterbalance the common urges to ignore the issues that made the difference between you and your ex-partner. These urges to rejoin your ex-partner are inappropriate because they go against your summary want; that is, your desire to end the couple relationship. When you find yourself in times of despair asking yourself, "Why am I leaving this wonderful person?" answering with a negative attribution can do the trick: "Because he is a controlling, selfish bum."

But there is some risk in talking and thinking about the negative aspects of your ex-partner. Sally pointed out that when her relationship got ugly towards the end, she was angry at both her ex-husband and herself. She didn't like herself when she was being negative; it whittled away at her self-esteem. It is important to recognize that the use of negative attribution and blaming, though they may be a useful way of dealing with the whirlwind of feelings in the moment, may have negative long-term effects on your self-esteem and the possibility of the friendship.

Joan summed up her experience from several relationships: *It never got ugly with the men who are now friends. I always liked myself, even when I was angry in the context of the breakup.*

Being negative and blaming your ex-partner in his or her presence can be dangerous. Doing so can assault his or her self-esteem and make more difficult the process of withdrawal from the relationship. With this in mind, if you decide to use this negative approach, you might best think the thoughts but not speak them aloud.

A couple of suggestions about the appropriate use of negative attribution in the transition: First, it is possible to "think it" but not to "believe it." That is, since we live in a constructed world, we can use our thoughts and perspectives on the world without becoming absorbed by them and mistaking them for reality.

Second, remember that it is the *behavior* of your ex-partner that you are defining as not okay, and not the person him- or herself. "It is your behavior that I don't like, but you are not a bad person," you may want to add.

Shiloh had decided to break off her relationship with Fredrico because he was abusively using drugs and repeatedly failing to meet his commitments to her. He frequently missed dinner parties and theatre performances. While Shiloh understood that the reasons for Fredrico's actions were complex and deeply rooted, she knew that she did not want to continue to suffer the disappointments of the broken commitments. So she said to him that she did not hate him as a person but rather simply could no longer tolerate his behavior.

## Move Beyond the Myth of Simple Ambivalence

The divorce recovery literature often portrays people in the process of breaking up as feeling simply "ambivalent" about the relationship as a whole. Perhaps unintentionally, and in response to our desires for a quick fix, they raise issues and ask questions that appear to only recognize two conflicting feelings. That is, an extremely complex set of decisions is made to appear to be the straightforward search for a yes or no answer. Consciously or unconsciously accepting this notion of simple ambivalence, however, can lead to an unnecessary additional sense of frustration and failure in the working-through process. This frustration and attendant strain can be avoided by accepting that the experience is much more complex.

While it is true that, with respect to some decisions (e.g., to actually separate or not), you will rely on your summary evaluation and experience yourself choosing a simple yes or no. However, beneath this decision is much processing which requires more awareness of the complexities of the situation.

To move beyond the limited view of ambivalent feelings means that you should consider more than simply, "Do I want this relationship or not?" In fact, a myriad of decisions must be made and must continue to be evaluated as you go through the process of change in the transition from lovers to friends. For example you might need to decide

1. What kinds of conversations do I want with him or her?
2. What do I want in the way of physical contact at this time?
3. Can I accept his or her use of alcohol?
4. Do I like the way we spend our time together?
5. How much change or in what areas will it take for me to continue to feel comfortable in the relationship?

Each time that you evaluate these and other concerns more specific to your own situation, they will have a different weight in terms of their importance for the continuation and form of the relationship. Nevertheless, you do have choices.

Another way in which your decisions are complex is that the meaning and value you place on any one issue is related to how that issue fits into the larger picture of your relationship. The importance of any one item on your list of choices is to some extent dependent upon how you or your ex-partner has handled other issues of importance. For example, whether you feel that your conversations with John are helpful at any given time may be connected to how you decide to spend your time together or whether he has honored another commitment. And the weight of these issues will be different for each person.

Actually the situation is even more complex. As you evaluate each of these facets of the relationship you are also deciding how you would feel about the relationship if one or all of the issues of concern changed. If Paula is upset with Walter for five different reasons she will in some way ask him to change. If he does change in one area she may feel differently about the others. For example, if Walter stops drinking, perhaps the way he spends money will be of less importance to Paula.

Each decision you make about the relationship is not just a matter of what you want or don't want, but what and how much you will accept in the context of the whole relationship.

What I've just said about the complex questions of what kind of a friendship you will have also applies to the prior process of evaluating whether or not to *remain* a couple as well. So whether you have already decided to separate or are deciding, it is important to recognize the real complexity of the matter. Recognizing that everything is in flux will help you avoid feelings of incompetence.

## Create a New and Improved Sense of Personal Identity

Your own personal identity, or how you know yourself to be, is related to how you see yourself in relation to others. When your relationship changes, a change in the way you view yourself must follow. Personal identity is important because who you are serves as the basis for what you want. Since in a transition period you must make many decisions about what you want, your personal identity, which may be less clear, becomes more important.

Even though we hear the word *identity* just about every day of our lives, most people are hard put to define it, and are unaware of the impact of their self-identity on their daily lives. Our definition of "self-identity" here will be "that which we perceive ourselves to be." For example, I am a writer, a therapist, father, mate, and a taxpayer. These aspects of my identity are actually *roles* that I have elected to play (though not without encouragement from others—like the IRS).

In addition to roles like these are more intimate aspects of our self-identity which are not so apparent to others and often unrevealed to ourselves as well. We are people who believe ourselves to be a good person (or bad), strong (or weak), elegant (or clumsy), emotionally balanced (or dependent upon others).

You might be a person of many moods, who likes certain kinds of music, has certain skills, and experiences specific fears and anxieties in your daily life. These are all aspects of personal identity. Many of these characteristics of your self-identity are ever apparent to you, though others may shape your experience only unconsciously. Whether you are conscious of these views of yourself or not, your every action is to some extent affected by your self-identity.

Your sense of self-identity is formed by your relationship with others, especially by your relationships with intimates. When you break up with a loved one you are left without those elements of your self-identity that were connected to your ex-partner. This can be good news and bad news. Maybe your partner frequently complained about your sexual performance, enough that you came to identify yourself as sexually inadequate. The loss of the relationship may in fact allow you to give up the notion that you are sexually inadequate and lead you to ultimately say, "I am a sexually okay person." If, on the other hand, you lose your belief that you are an important teammate at work, a valued mother, a relied-upon confidant, you will no doubt be less thrilled at the loss of these aspects of your personal identity. Much of the disappointment and emptiness at the breakup is related to the fact that you can no longer point to these esteem-building parts of your personal identity.

Faced with the void in your personality created by the change in circumstance, you may either fall into a state of disorientation and despair or take the opportunity to discover a new, emerging identity. Asked what you want in this situation, your only answer may be "I don't know." This is because the "I" in the "I don't know" is your self-identity which is now in disarray. The pain, anxiety, and confusion associated with your sudden awareness that you've lost aspects of your self-identity result in part because so much of how you see yourself lies beneath the surface of your consciousness. As Megan so beautifully put it,

*People handle [the balance] differently. He could keep seeing me. For me, I need some physical space. Because there's both an emotional transition and a physical transition. It's confusing because the feelings are sometimes in conflict. It felt to me like there was really a physiological experience of being together, sleeping together, that I missed over and above my emotional connection to him. When I was with him I literally walked differently, talked differently, moved in every way differently. Not being that way takes some getting used to.*

Particularly in the early stages of the breakup you can help yourself rebuild your sense of self-identity by using the following hints:

1. Look for those parts of your self-identity which emerged from your relationship with your partner. Notice not only the positive aspects of your couple-based self-identity but also any negative ones, such as "I am not a very good lover."

2. Acknowledge the loss of these aspects of your self-identity and grieve them as you grieve other aspects of the relationship. Or, in the case of the loss of negative self attributions, celebrate the loss!

3. Develop an inventory of other aspects of your self-identity which were not associated with your ex-partner. Write a list of responses completing the sentence which begins:

    "Unrelated to my relationship with _____, I know myself to be _____."

4. Take time to lie on your back in the sun, perhaps near a cool stream, and begin to envision a new view of yourself. Include in it your vision of yourself as a person who can successfully navigate the loss of parts of an important relationship. What do you want to see in yourself?

5. Try out new ways of acting and thinking to see how they feel.

In the study *When Marriage Ends*, Nicky Hart says that in "examining the length of time between separation and divorce, some people took months or years to rule out the possibility of reconciliation." In part this was because they could not figure out what or who they would be if they weren't in the old relationship. "In some cases it was not until the individual finalized some other

▼

plans for the future, in the shape of a new partner or in some cases a new occupational career that the old life could be abandoned."[8] For "new partner" or "new occupational career" we might read "development of new parts to self-identity."

As Stephanie, a twenty-three-year-old student, pointed out, *One way of helping each other is by each acting in your own interest. By doing this you free the other of the hope of reunion and thus assist them in letting go of the couple relationship.*

And Sean, a thirty-five-year-old architect, remarked: *I think it really worked that we were each doing something [working on a new sense of self] for ourselves. Things got clearer for both of us.*

When you are struggling to develop a new and improved sense of self-identity, a positive approach which will speed things along is to frequently try something new. Meet new friends, try to appreciate new art, music, and foods.

A natural tendency when working on developing a new self-identity is to say who you are *not* or what you do *not* want. This negative approach to establishing your new self-identity can actually be helpful when you are having difficulty generating positive ideas. However, you must take care not to get stuck in this "terrible twos" strategy; use it sparingly.

While this process of developing can be difficult and frustrating, you can also appreciate the fact that if your eyes are open you will see yourself in the making. Often in early relationships we fail to recognize that we are taking on aspects of our self-identity and thus sometimes mistakenly accept a view of ourselves that later, seeing through the eyes of experience, we find unacceptable. With your eyes open you can choose who you want to become, placing yourself more fully in command. You will feel proud of your accomplishment.

Recognizing that your self-identity is formed by the way the important people in your life view you and act toward you, of course, suggests that to build a good self-identity you must choose your friends wisely. Look for those who will support you as the person you would like to be.

## Emotionally Realign Yourself; Find Alternative Sources for Meeting Your Interpersonal Needs

Intimate personal relationships not only contribute to our sense of personal identity, but of course are an important source of emotional fulfillment. They let us feel cared for, supported, and nurtured. This section will define emotional needs and discuss ways to meet these needs both inside and outside of the changed ex-couple relationships.

Most recent books on surviving the breakup experience discuss the importance of working through the *emotional divorce*. That is, from their point of view, you must break off your emotional, intimate connection with your ex-partner. But this can be a distorted idea of what is actually possible. For example, Isolina Ricci emphatically states that "divorce means a definite—even if slow —ending of that intimacy" that constituted the original married relationship.[9] But a statement like this one mistakes for "intimacy" significant aspects of the married relationship which do not represent intimacy but rather habits of relatedness. In her "test" [of] intimacy" she asks, "Do you ever find yourself calling the other parent [of your child] 'my wife' or 'my husband' in conversation or in your thoughts?"; and "How often do you find yourself thinking about the other parent during a typical week?" Certainly, the more you can free yourself of these old images the better off your new relationships will be, but this does not mean that you are more or less intimate. Many of my interviewees told me that in many ways they felt freed to be more intimate with each other after they separated. They were more open, more willing to listen to the other, more caring, and more able to take the interests of the other to heart.

What is necessary in order to survive the breakup and maintain the friendship is not emotional divorce but what I call *emotional realignment*. You need not resign yourself into complete loss of intimacy with your ex-partner, but must come to enjoy a new form of intimacy which contains some new elements and is devoid of some of the couple-related ones.

Emotional realignment is a two-step process in which you first identify your emotional needs and then discover alternative ways in which these needs can be met by other persons or situations. For example, you may recognize that you long for your ex-partner to be constantly present. When you look up from the table at night and he or she is not there you may feel lonely and in need of contact with another. Instead of reaching for the phone to call your ex-mate, you can call a friend, or work on an engaging project that gives you pleasure and a sense of connectedness to others.

A common objection to this two-step method, particularly to asking for needs to be met by others is, "But it's so mechanical and cold. How can I just ask someone to meet my needs?" Each individual's reasons for feeling uncomfortable asking directly for what he or she wants or needs may be complex, different, and worth pursuing in individual therapy. But taking risks is a necessary evil which must be endured.

As part of the breakup process, you may have identified particular needs or wants of yours which were not met by your partner and which contributed to your desire to discontinue the relationship. If you have not already begun to seek out other resources for meeting these needs, do it now!

Because we lead so much of our daily life on automatic pilot, you may be having difficulty with the first step in the realignment process: identifying your needs and wants. Use the following need/want identification exercise to (1) identify your needs; (2) prioritize those that are most important; (3) evaluate each of these needs that were, or were not, being met in the couple relationship, and decide which can safely be met by your ex-partner within the realm of friendship after the breakup; (4) identify either alternative people through whom you can meet these interpersonal needs, or alternative actions you can take for yourself. In the third item above, the word *safely* means that you can have the need met by your ex-partner without damaging the boundary you have decided to establish between you. Test it by seeing whether you can answer *yes* to this question: "Can I turn to _____ for this need without losing sight of the fact that we are now friends and not a couple?"

## The Need/Want Identification Exercise[10]

**Step 1:** Read the following list of needs and place a check mark beside those which you feel to be important to you. The list is not meant to be exhaustive but rather to indicate some of the many needs you might have. Write down additional needs you can identify that are unique to you and your situation on the blank lines at the end of the following list.

In my relationships with others I need and want:
**trust and to be trusted**
**emotional support**
**physical affection**
**to be sexually valued and acknowledged**
**to be valued as a mate**

connection with family members
an opportunity to parent children
financial security
relationship security
to share ideas
to feel familiar
open conversation
acceptance
humor in tough times
similar religious beliefs
romance
someone who can make lasagne

_____

_____

_____

_____

_____

At the same time that you are emotionally realigning yourself with your ex-partner you can begin to seek out other ways to connect and other people with whom to connect. Through these new associations, with emotional integrity blazing the trail, you can find new ways to feel whole and fulfilled, even as you become single.

**Step 2:** Now that you have begun to identify what you need and want, make a list of all the people in your life whom you particularly value. This is not necessarily a list of close friends and family, but should include each person with whom you have meaningful contact.

To some extent this emotional realignment will be forced on you whether you like it or not. In a breakup, individuals may lose something they need from a relationship, such as caring for children, which may be something that is important to self worth. When a change in circumstances means that you can't care for your children regularly, you are left in a *deficit* situation.[11] That is, an aspect of your life which has become necessary for you to feel complete is missing.

Zack remembered the first several months after his separation from his wife. He found himself standing at the kitchen sink of his new apartment in the morning feeling at a loss. During his marriage this had been the time that he was hurriedly helping his kids get ready for school. As he stared out the window, he realized that he could not think of anything to do with this time and that he felt a large emotional hole where his role as a parent to his children had been.

If you are experiencing a persistent sense of incompleteness, *know thy weaknesses;* avoid the common tendency of looking to your ex-partner or your children to meet your needs at a stage when it is inappropriate. This is the time to seek out the support of other friends and family or find other activities. Redirect yourself this way to correct your sense of being in a *deficit* situation emotionally.

## Move Beyond Mere *Functioning* to Creativity and the Freedom to Choose What You Want for Yourself and Your Relationship

As I have said, caring for yourself in the interest of self *and* the friendship means acting in a creative way to build a new you rather than reacting to the predictable pressures toward fatalistic despair.

During the period of disorientation and suspension of emotions which often follows the breakup, many people remark that their goal is to simply be able to function like their old selves. While this survivalist attitude may be necessary in the very early chaotic phases, it is important to begin the process of transition with the goal of a better more complete and fulfilling life, rather than of simply functioning.

In the postbreakup period, as you begin to develop a better sense of who you want to be in the future, you will soon discover that to *act* upon your thoughts is as important as to have them in the first place. It is important to *act* on your new image to remind yourself of who you are becoming and to believe that you are, indeed, becoming who you want to be.

Strengthen your efforts to change by writing personal notes of commitment to yourself. For example, when you are feeling good about yourself you may recognize that an important part of your effort to grow is to spend some time each day alone. With this in mind you might write yourself a note saying, "Remember *for yourself*: spend a small amount of time each day alone." Write your messages to yourself in a supportive, positive tone. Negative statements tend to keep you preoccupied with the behavior and attitudes you want to change, while they simultaneously tear down your self-esteem.

As an example of the way in which positive language is more helpful than negative language, an acquaintance once told me that while he had attempted to quit smoking many times, he had always failed because he "couldn't stop thinking about smoking when I was trying to control myself and not smoke." After analyzing his predicament he had devised an ingenious plan for defeating his ability to defeat himself. On the day he wanted to

▼

quit he decided that he would begin doing *everything* differently, not just stopping smoking. So he got up on the opposite side of the bed; he buttoned his shirt with the opposite hand; ate pancakes for breakfast (which he hated). He reported that he soon had no interest in smoking again! If you have ever attempted to quit smoking or any other significant habit, you might remember that by telling yourself that you don't want to smoke you are giving yourself a constant reminder of something you don't want to think about. Thus for example, you might write the following list:

## Ideas for commitment: Do the following:

**1.** Spend one hour a day doing something that I really enjoy.

**2.** Make an effort to listen when he/she talks rather than trying to change the situation too quickly.

**3.** Call a friend to talk over any actions that might not be in the interest of the new me.

**4.** Find something each day that I have done well.

**5.** Stand my ground when he/she calls and wants me to come over to fall in love again.

**6.** Look for opportunities to act differently in each new situation I find myself in.

You can use these notes as guidelines for action during those tough times as well, as a way of constructing a new reality.

The transition from lovers to friends *can be* an arduous one requiring a significant commitment. As you read the next chapter I hope you will think of working together with your ex-partner in such a way that both of you gain in strength and energy.

▼

# 6

# HELPING EACH OTHER
# TRANSITION TO FRIENDSHIP

▼

1. What can your ex-partner do to make the transition to friendship after the breakup more possible?
2. What specific agreements about the ways you act toward each other can make the transition to friendship easier for *you*. For *your ex-partner?*
3. What are the current obstacles getting in the way of your growing postbreakup friendship?
4. What makes the time that you spend with your ex-partner more comfortable for *you?*

Just as there are individual coping issues within the breakup process, there are issues that confront the ex-couples involved. I hope that you noticed in the previous sentence that it is assumed that regardless of the nature of the relationship, ex-partners *will* have some kind of relationship. It is simply up to the individuals involved to decide *what kind* of relationship it will be. While not all the participants of my study were aware of it at the time of the breakup, they acknowledged that they wanted, to one degree or another, a friendly relationship with their former partner.

Let's remain focused on the positive and constructive aspects of relationship evolution, i.e., those actions and attitudes which have helped others before you in making a successful and gratifying transition from lovers to friends. Behind each action or attitude, envision the underlying problem or issue it addresses and tailor your use of these suggestions to your own situation.

## Important Dimensions of Friendship

Before describing the ways in which ex-partners can be helpful to each other and move towards a postbreakup friendship, I would like to call your attention to several general aspects of relationships that you must keep in mind. In all relationships there is a positive need for limit setting. Friendship is a living action subject to constant change. Time and timing play a powerful role in the success of relating. Relationships have a natural complexity and uniqueness that make general rules difficult to ascertain. Active change is a joint effort with individual discretion. Communication is an important time-proven key to success.

### Limit Setting

Whenever I broach the notion of setting limits in relationships, someone invariably complains that saying *no* (i.e., setting a firm limit of any kind) will surely destroy any chance for a relationship because it implies that you are selfish or simply do not care. Actually, the situation is quite the opposite. Peter Schellenbaum in *How to Say No to the One You Love*, points out that saying no is vital for the relationship to survive because without the loving *no* there can be no loving *yes* of any value.[1] By this he means that love relationships need a balance of separateness and togetherness to remain clear and vital.

Relationships are dialectic. They oscillate between opposites and the synthesis of opposites, such as striving for intimacy and connectedness while striving for detachment and distance. We tend to think that couple relationships move only in one direction: toward increasing intimacy. This one-directional and one-dimensional view is partly responsible for our inability to accept that couple relationships can and do change in an infinite variety of directions with a breakup. Thus, if you can accept this "oscillating" view of your relationship—that both intimacy and detachment are of value to you and the relationship—you will recognize that making the transition from lovers to friends is not a matter of simply accepting less intimacy, but is rather a process of changing the amount and the nature of intimacy and detachment as you construct your new friendship.

It is essential that you learn to set caring limits and learn to give from a position of strength and generosity without fear in the relationship.

## Friendship as a Living Action

*Friendship* and *relationship* are constantly changing. While the dictionary tells us that the words *friendship* and *relationship* are defined as nouns—as *objects* or *things*, not changing processes—that doesn't hold true for relationships. But because we tend to *nominalize*, or make these concepts static rather than active vital processes for the sake of communication, we also tend to forget that all of life is really a process, including the "friending," relating, loving, and hating.

The suggestions offered below can help you go through the process, depending on the (changing) nature of the relationship you are working on at the time. What works today may not work tomorrow, and vice versa.

## Time and Timing

As I interviewed people for this book, I was frequently reminded of the importance of time and timing. Answers to almost all of the questions I asked differed depending upon where the couple or the individuals were in their relationship. For example, when I asked, "How long was it before you knew it was time to begin rebuilding your new friendship?" the answers ranged from "immediately after the decision to break up" to "ten years." The length of time was determined by a variety of issues related to the individual, the couple, the people around them, and the spirit of the moment.

## Natural Complexity and Uniqueness

All relationships, especially friendships, are multifaceted and complex. The contour of the relationship is varied and fragile, like a broken jagged glass. This can be both exciting and frustrating. For example, you and your ex-partner may easily agree on some of the ways you want or don't want to be together. You both might readily agree that it is too difficult and dangerous to be with each other in certain circumstances—for example, to sleep in the same bedroom in the early stages of the breakup process. You might differ on whether meetings should take place on neutral territory for the purpose of making the newly forming friendship feel safe.

When asked, "How long did it take before you felt comfortable in the new relationship?" one person replied "It's really hard to say. Some things, like talking on the phone, were easy right away. Meeting for lunch in an old favorite restaurant took much longer."

Her ex-partner said, "The only real hard part for me was seeing her with someone else. So I asked that we meet privately for a while."

## Active Change Is a Joint Effort and Individual Right

Each person has the opportunity to change the friendship and to define what it will be like. If one ex-partner wants to meet for lunch and the other does not, meeting for lunch is simply out of the question. There is little to be gained by attempting to talk the other person into conforming to your every desire. Besides, what will not work today may, to you and your ex-partner's surprise, be effortless in a week.

## Communication as a Worn but Still-Working Key

There are essentially three important points of view of the relationship: yours, your ex-partner's, and the one you construct together. When you reach an impasse in the growth of the friendship it is often because one or more of these points of view differs from the others. If so, it's time to talk and get clear.

The way in which you communicate is as important as the act or intent to communicate. If you have not been exposed to the wealth of information available in the form of workshops, seminars, and books, dealing with authentic, effective communication, I encourage you to seek this information out now. A few elements of the kind of effective communication that will be helpful in your efforts to transition from lovers to friends follow:

**Use "I" Statements.** Because the demons of guilt and blame are so active during the breakup of a relationship, it is essential for successful transitioning that you *own* your feelings. To *own* your feelings means acknowledging that if you are feeling angry, sad, hurt, etc., it is because *you* choose to feel that way; your ex-partner cannot *make* you feel anything. While it is true that if one's partner has an affair, most people would feel some combination of hurt, sadness, and anger, they would feel that way *not* because of the behavior but because they chose to make it important when they committed themselves to the relationship.

The best way to *own* your feelings is to consistently use the "I" statement format when you talk about your feelings. For example, you might say, "I feel angry at the fact that you went out with Jane behind my back!" Compare this with the form of the sentence when you are *not* owning your feelings: "You *made* me angry when you went out with Jane!" Notice that in the latter sentence form there is a blaming tone (whether it is deserved or not) which will almost invariably put your ex-partner on the defensive. This will effectively torpedo any further meaningful communication. People can't listen well from a defensive position because they are too preoccupied with the security operation of attempting to salvage their self-esteem.

**Active Listening.** When listening to what others are saying, particularly in emotionally charged situations, it is often difficult to *hear* what the other is saying because you are too absorbed in *thinking* about what you want to say next. If you don't *hear* what each other is saying, you are not communicating even if you are both talking. More accurately, you will be engaged in parallel monologues. This can be frustrating and destructive to your friendship.

One way to assure that you at least hear what the other person is saying (even if you don't agree) is to use the skills of *active listening*. The essential ingredients of active listening are *paraphrasing, clarifying,* and *giving feedback.*

*Paraphrasing* means that when your partner says something, you quickly state in your own words what you *think* the person just said. I emphasize the word *think* because when you paraphrase what your partner has just said, it is equally important to listen to his or her response to learn whether or not your understanding was correct.

*Clarifying* is deceptively straightforward, particularly when the situation is tense. In clarifying you will try to get a clearer picture of what your ex-partner is trying to communicate by asking questions until you are both satisfied that you heard what was being said. You must, however, take care that your questioning of your partner is only for the purpose of gaining understanding and not a disguised way of making a negative statement. The "Are you just the kind of person who can't make a commitment?" question is a good example of a statement being passed off as a question.

*Feedback* is your opportunity to respond to what you have just heard and let your feelings about it be known. For the future of the friendship it is important that you avoid being judgmental in giving feedback.

**The Power of What You Say.**   What you say and the way in which you say it will have a profound impact not only upon your partner but on the way in which you yourself think. Isolina Ricci points out in her book *Mom's House, Dad's House* that the language we use in the divorce or breakup can determine the outcome of our efforts to build a new relationship. If you describe the change taking place in your relationship as "a failed relationship" you will have difficulty avoiding the need to blame each other. Saying that the relationship has ended "as it was" or that "we are simply changing our relationship" will undoubtedly leave you both open to more options but might be unrealistic. You will have to struggle to achieve a balance.

Not only do words define your status with each other in ways that either enhance or detract from your chances for a positive relationship, but words can also unnecessarily perpetuate ill feeling and make intimate contact painful.

*What* you say is also important. If, in the heat of discussion you use intimate knowledge about your ex-partner as a way of gaining power over the conversation, the level of pain and mistrust you engender may have long-lasting, debilitating effects on your relationship. For example, if your ex-partner has previously told you that he or she fears commitment to the relationship you must be careful not to use this information to prove that he or she is the source of the breakup.

## Helping Each Other Remain Friends

When asked their advice on what ex-partners could do for each other to make the transition from lovers to friends easier, the interviewees discovered that it was difficult to distinguish between helping themselves, helping their ex-lovers, and helping their relationship. What they did for the friendship was often to work on their own personal issues. To clarify distinctions between those types of helping, this section will focus on helpful actions directed toward ex-partners or toward the friendship between them.

To help each other, try the following:

1. Don't accept the problem point of view.
2. Act *as if* you are friends even if your feelings are not quite there.
3. Clean up the relationship.
4. Agree on and support each other's sexual needs in the relationship.
5. Help each other handle the emotional withdrawal and dependence.
6. Be cautious in accepting the advice of friends and family.
7. Be there for each other.
8. Develop a mutually acceptable account of the demise of the relationship to present to the world.
9. Give each other the gift of distance when it is needed.
10. Be prepared to handle the introduction of new partners into each of your lives.

11. Be supportively honest.
12. Avoid excessive positive statements in the beginning of the transition to friendship, such as complimenting the other's appearance or ability to cope.

## Don't Accept Only the Problem-Focused Approach to the Relationship—Take a Proactive Approach

Be aware of, and ready for, common areas of conflict that might emerge in the transition period. Conflict areas can include property distribution, physical contact, shared friends, control over conversation, time together, and what subjects are okay to discuss. It's easy to prepare yourself with stock responses: "If she gets too emotional, I'll just leave"; "If he tries to touch me I'll tell him I have a right to control my own body"; "I know she's going to try to trick me into getting back together so I'll confront her each time she tries it." But focusing on problems in this way might actually make a successful transition more difficult than necessary.

While burying your head in the sand won't make the problems, conflicts, and worries go away, taking the defensive problem point of view approach to surviving the breakup can lead down a road you may not want to travel.

When you actively look for the darkness in the relationship in this manner, you increase your feelings of despair and hopelessness. Thoughts and feelings of hope and success cannot dominate from this perspective. True, you may need to focus on the negative for a while to help create emotional distance—to say to yourself, "Who would want to be with such a jerk?" "My ex is an insensitive clod," etc. But see if you can recognize the need for the distance, and state it and act on it more directly.

Another reason for avoiding the problem-focused approach is that there is an economy of effort in coping with the transition process. The total amount of time and energy in life is limited, like the money in our bank account. Obsessing on problems takes time and energy away from your efforts to create, or positively construct, or plan the new friendship you hope to achieve. Try to balance your awareness of both positive constructions and of possible conflicts. As Marlene so poignantly stated:

*I think what made the transition easier for us was that we both were committed to building a new relationship. We knew we would be friends forever. Sure, there were difficult times but that was not what we want to get stuck on. We wanted to find a way to succeed.*

## Use Positive Language

You can each contribute to a more constructive transition process by stating your wishes in positive language. I don't mean *positive* in the sense of good or nice, here. Rather, *positive* in the sense of telling the other person (or yourself internally) what you want rather than what you don't want. By contrast, this is a negative statement to your ex-partner:

*Don't call me so often; it makes me really upset.*

You can more effectively phrase your desires in a positive, directive statement such as:

*Because I am having difficulty with my feelings about you, I would appreciate it if you would call me just twice a week.*

In the best of scenarios, when you are at the beginning stages of breaking up, you could jointly affirm the way in which you would like to handle the relationship by writing a statement. You can do this either by working together or separately, later combining the results. If you are having difficulty constructing such a paragraph because you are overwhelmed with negative feelings, you might like to use the following breakup manifesto, ver-batim, as a temporary guide until you're ready to create your own.

*We both know that we are facing difficult feelings because we are breaking up. In spite of these feelings we know that some parts of our relationship are important to us both. I, Jack, value you, Jill, because [insert one positive appreciation you have for your ex-partner]. Because we still value each other we will make every effort to (1) spend one hour per week talking about what we are experiencing with each other, (2) state our requests in a positive way, (3) agree to allow one another to take "time out" whenever we want to.*

Over time, you will want to add to the statements as your situation changes.

## Act *As If* You Are Friends

From her experience, Beth pointed out, "The most important thing to be kept in mind is that you must treat each other *as if* you are friends." Behind her statement is the fact that she has created in her mind a positive view of what she would like her relationship with her ex-partner to be. This image then serves as a guide to her future actions.

When asked, most people offer similar definitions of friend-ship and of the ideal traits of a true friend—being trustworthy, caring, willing to listen, willing to give and take, and accepting of who the other is. Actually the ways in which you build your own self-esteem can serve as a guide for what you can do for your ex.

Friends are gently honest, able to say yes and no, and to treat you respectfully. Ellen, a thirty-year-old fine artist, and her ex-partner, Sal, both found that they were often at a loss for what to say to each other as ex-partners. With the help of a therapist, each was able to describe the way in which he or she would like to be treated as a friend. As Ellen commented later,

*For me, it was important during the change period that when things got difficult, we really acted as if we were friends. You know, when there are hard things to say you say them because you know they need to be said and you trust that your friend can handle them.*

**Using Humor.** The value of humor in lightening unbearable situations in relationships does not get enough press. You are likely to blunder with some frequency in the transition from lovers to friends, given that the tasks are often difficult and you are without models to guide you. At these times you can help each other by agreeing to give each other the space to make mistakes. One way to do this is to carefully and caringly use humor.

Sue and Allie, two clients of mine who are ex-lovers, offer a great example. For several weeks, our therapy sessions had mirrored the extremely tense, anger-laden interactions which plagued them at home. While we all knew that there was something beneath the anger and bickering, we just couldn't identify it. All kinds of assumptions were being made and acted upon with little thought. To slow this process down, I suggested that they each go home and act as though they were new friends. As new friends, they would be expected to *ask* whenever they wanted anything from each other. They were also told to *not* talk about anything of any importance. They agreed. When they got home Sue thought that Allie was about to talk about something controversial. Spontaneously, she raised her hands in front of her and made the sign of the cross as if she were warding off an evil spirit. They both burst into laughter. Each uses this humorous invention, which for them means, "I love you but I don't want to fight right now." After a couple of weeks of respite they were ready to face some of the more difficult underlying issues. Because of this humorous intervention they also had a good dose of friendly interactions to support them.

Of course, the use of humor can be as dangerous as it can be helpful. Remember to give it the, "How-would-I-feel-if-he-or-she-said-this-to-me test" before saying what's on your mind.

## Clean Up the Relationship

Many interviewees said that it was very important to "clean up the relationship." In part, this meant to spend time with each other trying to understand in a nonjudgmental way what happened, to tie up the loose ends—unfinished business.

Cleaning up also means such things as communicating your feelings and concerns with friends and family of the ex-partner about the change in the relationship and the meaning of these changes for your relationships with them. Often in-laws and partner-related friends have become a very important part of each of your lives. The clarification and reaffirmation of these peripheral relationships can be an important supportive context for the ex-couple's friendship as well as their individual well-being.

## Agree Upon and Support Each Other's Attempts to Control the Sexual Part of the Relationship

Sexual intimacy between partners and the way they feel about themselves sexually are commonly such powerful issues that they can be the Achilles' heel of the friendship enterprise. Assisting each other in coping with the confusing feelings of sexual attraction is therefore generally an essential part of managing the breakup transition.

Perhaps the most common problem in romantic relationships is that of differences in sexual desire. Sexual desire discrepancy, both in terms of the frequency and the type of desired sexual contact, emerges from a variety of sources. To fully under-stand the sources of discrepancies between partners you have to look at their personal history extending back to the birth family attitudes, religious ideas, personal sexual identity, as well as actual experience of sexual contact. To be sure, the role that sexuality plays in relationships and in the breakup process varies greatly from couple to couple, but for none is it a nonissue.

For those couples that broke up for reasons other than sex-ual dissatisfaction, managing physical attraction and sexual con-tact after the breakup is perhaps one of the most difficult tasks. All the extremely good reasons which led them to break up can seem to simply evaporate in the heat of sexual passion. Unfortu-nately, in all but a few cases, an increased sense of despair and depression follows each sexual contact after the breakup.

Interestingly enough, among those couples for which their sexual relationship was very problematic while they were a cou-ple, many find that their sexual relationship improved after they broke up. In some cases when difficult aspects of "being a couple" were removed, such as intimacy, the need to share power in many areas, not enough focused time together, the partners' desire to be sexual and their ability to enjoy being sexual improved dra-matically.

The issue of sexual intimacy is particularly important be-cause for some people, seemingly more so for men than for women, sex is one major way in which they allow themselves to be truly intimate and vulnerable.

For Mary, the few sexual contacts she has had with her ex-lover were a source of comfort in the midst of other difficult times.

*I felt lonely, and filled with anxiety. So when I went to be with him we made love. I knew that we would not become a couple again but being sexual gave me a feeling of comfort.*

The issue of sexual intimacy can also be very highly charged. In a pre-interview discussion, Sheri volunteered that her seductive ties with her ex-partner inhibited her desire to maintain a friendship:

*I feared that the boundary that we were struggling to maintain would fall at any time. That's part of why I knew he didn't really want to be true friends. He kept pushing me for a sexual affair, even when he was in another relationship. He knew I wanted him but he also knew it was hurting me. That's not the way a friend acts.*

As Megan so beautifully described, even the meaning of the sexual part of the relationship can also change after the breakup:

*The meaning of sex is different after you have emotionally decided that it's over. One time with Ray, when we went to bed after we broke up, it wasn't the same as when we were together but it was kind of a healing experience. It brought closure to that part of the relationship. It dispelled any illusion that there was more to the relationship.*

Sexual contact after the breakup is important not only because of the way these difficult feelings have to be managed but also because the way in which it is handled will have an impact upon other relationships too. Stephanie hit the nail on the head:

*Sex after the breakup can make the transition more difficult. It's like it points to a big void there. If we are physically intimate it makes it difficult to have the desire to create new romantic relationships and thereby stops you from moving ahead.*

Okay, so what can couples do to help each other manage their sexual relationship?

**Talk about It.** First and foremost, it is essential that you help each other manage your sexual behavior by taking the time and risking talking about what you are experiencing. Good, esteem-building communication can be the key to handling these often-excruciating issues. If you are direct about your mixed feelings (in a caring way), the physical euphoria that might otherwise sweep you away can be tempered with *reality*. And remember the old saying, "barking dogs don't bite"—because they're too busy barking. A little crude, but you get the point.

**A-Frame Hugs.** As part of your communication about your sexual relationship you can try to reach agreement about the structure of your physical contact—what you can tolerate, what you want. Randy, a human service worker, reported that he and his ex-partner had found a direct, unique solution to being physically close without unleashing uncontrollable sexual feelings. To salvage a sense of closeness and freedom to touch each other despite their annoying continued sexual attraction,

*We decided that neither of us could handle a close body hug but we knew we wanted to feel free to hug each time we met. We then agreed to the "A-frame" hug [hugging at the shoulders, but not pressing bodies together] as our solution. By maintaining that position we were able to get close but not unbearably and suggestively close.*

Be creative!

## Helping Each Other Cope with Emotional Dependence

Coping with the emotional dependence, the uncomfortable craving for the emotional support or connection with ex-partners, provokes the most confusing of interactions for ex-couples. Even though each individual must deal with the loss of valued emotional contact separately, there are mutually supportive ways to handle emotional contact and intimacy.

Use the section "Taking Care of Yourself" as a guide, too, to the issues and ways in which you can be helpful to your partner and to your friendship in coping with the withdrawal from your emotional dependence on each other.

This emotional dependence is shaped by (1) you and your partner's sense of identity and your ability to self-nurture, (2) the kind of relationship you had and the needs you met for each other, (3) the particular way in which you each meet your emotional needs.

We become emotionally dependent much in the same way that we become dependent upon others for our sense of identity. This dependency is to some extent particular to the person and what they mean to us, and is to some extent our habitual belief that someone else's way of understanding and caring for us is unique and irreplaceable. And to some extent dependency reflects the simple economy of consciousness: we become accustomed to having our mental and emotional space filled by another. Losing accustomed support is like riding a bicycle and having the pedal fall off: sometimes it's disappointing; sometimes it's painful.

**Rules for Transition.** Cold as it may sound, perhaps one of the most useful ways in which you can support each other through withdrawal from emotional dependence is to establish clear rules for the way in which you will interact. Jeff put it well:

*It's important that we don't dwell on the glorious past, at least for now. . . . Keep a consistent communication so that you have more than the past to talk about. Otherwise you are left with things being the way they were.*

The strategies earlier suggested for coping with sexual impulses and pain work here, too. Establish agreements about how you will behave in these areas:

**the amount of time you will spend together**
**the types of activities you will share**
**how you will conduct your joint relationships with other family and friends**

**finances**
**professional contacts**
**sharing joint belongings and property**
**issues that you are and are not willing to discuss**
**time to talk about the rules**

Of course, because your relationship is constantly changing, the rules will have to be constantly renegotiated. If the inability to negotiate aspects of the relationship may have been the basis for your breakup in the first place, you may find it helpful to seek out a therapist to assist you on an as-needed basis. When you approach your ex-partner for a lunch date and are unexpectedly refused, be aware that your ex-partner may be still attempting to develop a new way of looking at the relationship, and might find old haunts haunting.

Another way in which you can help support your ex-partner in coping with emotional dependence is to support his or her efforts to realign emotionally with other people. Certainly, a difficult part of the breaking up process is seeing your ex-partner with other people, particularly other prospective mates. Despite the pain that you will feel, it is essential that you at least not interfere even if you can't be supportive.

## Measure the Advice of Friends/Family

Listening to the people that I interviewed for this book, I was surprised at how little they felt that their friends or family had had an impact upon their lives as a couple, their decision to break up, or their relationship after the breakup. Perhaps this is why they actually could stay friends! Nevertheless, I know from my therapy practice that friends and family can have either very negative or very positive influence on the transition from lovers to friends.

Jackie, for example, pointed out that it was very difficult for her to stay on track with her desire to remain friends with her ex-partner in the face of the general attitudes of her family and friends.

*Even at the divorce support group people keep telling me that I'm crazy to try to stay friends with my ex. They say that it's just because I can't get over losing him. Sometimes it makes it very hard for me to stay confident that we can do it. My friends and family are just the same.*

Of course, the first thing to remember if you receive general disparaging remarks from friends or family is that the statistics about postdivorce relationships, your experience, and that of many others reported in this book, are increasingly proving them wrong.

Friends and family often feel a divided sense of loyalty that makes the advice that they give to either partner suspect. So caution is required when listening to other's opinions about your postbreakup friendship.

## Be There for Each Other
People who have more frequent contact with their ex-spouses are significantly more likely to feel friendly toward them than those who have less. Likewise, those who have less frequent contact are more likely to have more hostile feelings. While these findings do not directly mean that increased communication and contact will lead to more friendly feelings, some of the people that I interviewed felt that continued attempts to communicate with their ex were important for the existence and growth of their friendship.

Each of the participants who had a difficult time with the separation and breakup said that feeling alone was the most dif-

ficult aspect of the separating process. For them, being alone was not having the person there to be with in the old familiar ways and to have their needs for connection and caring met. Said one,
*The most difficult thing was to release the dependency. You grow so used to being with somebody. That was the hardest thing, to confront the starkness of being alone. I was right up against myself, with no one to console me.*

For Marie, the most difficult part of breaking up was
*not having someone there. The fact that we talked so much [when together] and then not having that person there to talk. Also, loss of the sexual activity.*

Several people mentioned that because their ex-partner is still one of the most intimate connections in their lives, just knowing that the other is available to be supportive is a help. Joan put it this way:
*You've spent years opening the door to another person. You let them come to you and you to go to them. Just because you're not together doesn't mean you shut the door.*

As you attempt to be there for the other, you'll need to maintain a proper balance of intimacy and distance, especially if it is soon after the breakup. Frequently monitor your motivation for being there. If you are making yourself available based upon feelings of guilt, pity, or avoidance of your own feelings of loss, you might be setting yourself up for a big disappointment. Your efforts to maintain the friendship will be made even more difficult if these disappointments pile up. Further, the resentment which often accompanies disappointment will also become an added burden. One participant suggested that ex-partners *listen to each other and still be supportive of almost whatever the person needs. We both know that it's still a very volatile situation but we also know that we want to be long-term friends. Knowing this helps a lot.*

## Develop a Mutually Acceptable Account of the Demise of the Relationship

In the process of breaking up, couples characteristically develop individual and mutual accounts or explanations of what they believe caused the breakup. These accounts have impact on their survival as individuals and as a couple who want to be friends. The account that an individual develops seems a relative truth, which he or she can accept without excessive damage to sense of self-esteem or hopefulness for the future. Everyone differs in the amount of personal responsibility he or she is willing to take, regardless of the "truth" of the matter. It is very important for each of you, as accurately as possible, to accept responsibility for your role in the demise of your relationship as well as your role in the development of the postbreakup friendship. Developing an individual account at least somewhat compatible with the mutual account you establish seems to be helpful in allowing you to put the breakup in its place and move on with your life. Each individual weighs the reasons for the breakup differently. For some the breakup itself may be a source of great embarrassment while for others it may simply be a disappointment. Diane Vaughn, in her book, *Uncoupling: Turning Points in Intimate Relationships,* says:

*Through the social process of mourning they, too, eventually arrive at an account that explains this unexpected denouement [of the relationship]. "Getting over" the relationship does not mean relinquishing the part of our life that we shared with another but rather coming to some conclusion which allows us to accept its altered significance. Once we develop such an account, we can incorporate it into our lives and then go on.[2]*

▼

The mutual account you give to the outside world also has a profound impact upon your efforts to maintain friendship. By *mutual* I mean that together you agree on the explanation that you will offer for your breakup to the world at large. Both the content of the account (*what* you actually decide to deliver to the world) and the process of developing the mutual account (the act of devising it and the way that you do it) are meaningful.

The process of creating a mutually acceptable account gives you a chance, as a couple, to (1) express your concerns, (2) understand your ex-partner's point of view without having to accept it as gospel, (3) offer each other support in coping with concerns about other people's attitudes about the breakup. As you develop your mutual account, you can anticipate that the process will be difficult, uncomfortable, and sometimes estranging because you will review what happened in the relationship. And of course these feelings emerge because disagreement about what happened or didn't happen in the relationship is often the original antagonism that precipitated your breakup in the first place.

The social circumstance of your lives will shape both the importance and the nature of the mutual account that you create as well as the way that you deliver it. Steve, an organizational consultant, shared a business with his ex-partner, so they needed something to say to their employees that would not only save face for each of them but would also avoid the possibility of disrupting their relationships with their employees.

*We not only developed a public story from ourselves to our employees but felt that it was important that they be clear about what they were supposed to share with the outside world—outside the company.*

He went on to say that this was one aspect of breaking up which they both felt that they had handled well; it was a source of pride which enhanced their mutual respect.

*I am very proud of the fact that Diane and I succeeded at something that almost nobody thought possible.*

If done well, the mutual account will allow you to continue your friendship more easily. If you clearly give the message that *we* decided to break up, you can more readily share your future lives in shared social space without the difficulty of one or the other being embarrassed.

## Give Each Other the Gift of Distance When It Is Needed

Sometimes your ex-partner will need you to be there, but it is just as important that you be willing and aware enough to give your ex-partner the gift of distance when he or she needs it. Elliot noted:

*When we first broke up I tried to talk with her a lot at work, partly because I wanted to keep the work situation mellow and partly because I just didn't want to be shut out. But every time I spoke to her it hurt so badly that I would almost be immobilized for days to come.*

Perhaps the only way to know whether it is better to be there or offer space at a particular time is to ask. This, too, is not utterly foolproof, because when you or your friend are in distress you don't always know what you want.

Particularly in times of difficult transition, everyone needs to feel that he or she is in control of their life. Pressures from ex-partners can complicate both individual change and adaptation as well as the re-creation of the new friendship. The power to call *time out* is essential. As one participant remarked,

*I think that it is probably necessary to go through a period, after the separation, of more distance and more conflict. You have to keep in mind that that's sort of a phase of adaptation to the new relationship. You've*

got to expect some period of time when you're less comfortable with each other. There will be more tension.

Commonly ex-partners will especially need to give each other time and space at the time of the breakup because the person who initiates separation is often ahead of the partner in making some of the emotional adjustments necessary to the process of disengaging. "Dumpees" say that it is important for them that their ex-partner understand that they need space and time.[3] Often when the "dumper" tries to be nice and takes care of them it made it harder to work through the emotional issue on which they were stuck. Dumpees have to get beyond the anger that is usually going to come up at some time during the breakup. What's important is that you accept that at some time in the future you will get beyond the anger and give each other the space you need for that anger to either be worked out privately or the emotional part of it diffused enough so that then you can come together to talk.

Another way in which leavers can help the cause of continued friendship is to understand and allow the often threatening emotions, worries, and pleadings voiced by their ex-partners. Listening to these expressions of despair *without leaping up to fix them* is valuable both in the short and the long term. Attempting to save your ex-partner from these intense feelings, on the other hand, will only prolong and perhaps worsen the experience.

Giving time and space often makes the one who leaves feel everything from guilt to fear to a kind of untouchable anxiety. In response to these feelings the leaver often feels a strong urge to attempt to rescue the other from his or her feelings of anger, disappointment, and loss by being overly sympathetic and giving. Ironically this rescue effort can make the experience even more difficult. It is hard for some individuals to make emotional prog-

▼

ress when their ex-partners are being too kind or too close because they feel an indebtedness that makes it harder to express
negative but natural feelings. You may not intend to say so, but
an underlying message conveyed by such rescue attempts is that
the ex-partner is weak and cannot be trusted to take care of him-
or herself. This is not only degrading but may lead to an even
lower sense of self-esteem.

So, if you are feeling the powerful pull within you to rejoin
your ex-partner (even against your ex-partner's or your best interest), the short and simple *I won't do it and I won't forget it* exercise
can help, particularly if you are in the early or middle stages of
the breakup.

**1.** Write down on a piece of paper the ways in which you
want to interact with your ex-partner in the moment. You might
want to do things for him or her, to express your love, offer your
support or assistance, or simply spend time together.

**2.** At the top of your list write the heading *"To be done when
we are ready."*

This simple two-step exercise is useful in at least three ways.
First, if you're writing and thinking about the list you cannot at
the same time be rescuing your ex-partner. Writing the list can
also help you understand yourself better: it shows you your definition of what you would like the relationship to be. This will
lead you to see when you are acting out of concern for your ex-
partner and when you are attempting to assuage some difficult
feeling of your own.

Finally, much of what makes us act on our impulses prematurely is that we are afraid of losing an important opportunity.
By entitling your list "To be done when we are ready" you can
stave off your fears that you will forget to act affirmatively on

these feelings and attitudes at the proper moment. Put the list in a safe place for use when the time is right.

## Be Prepared to Handle the Introduction of New Partners into Each of Your Lives

Coping with the arrival of new lovers in your partner's life is perhaps one of the most traumatic and discomforting experiences. Interestingly enough, many of those interviewed felt that it was liberating as well. Buddy showed that new partners may even give a significant boost to the transition from lovers to friends.

*I think it was very important to Dalia that she met Dick. That allowed her to and allowed us to be better friends. She met him after a year, and she felt that our relationship was really over.*

Handling the introduction of new partners suggests that you will need to assist your new partner to cope with his or her feeling about your prior relationship. The suggestions most frequently made by those who had successfully integrated their ex-partners into their new relationship were:

1. Make clear to your current partner that the relationship between the two of you is absolutely sacred.
2. Check out meetings with your ex-partner in advance, including type of meeting, place, timing.
3. Regularly check out your partner's feelings and concerns.
4. Do not withhold information from your partner that might seem threatening. On the other hand, be sure to ask your partner what he or she really wants to know.
5. Whenever possible introduce your new partners to your ex-partner. As one participant remarked, "Well of course, because they both know me, they have a high chance of

having something in common. I try to make the connection between them, sometimes using humor."

Find things they have in common and introduce them. It will be important to be present with your current partner and support his or her concerns.

6. Be clear within yourself about the nature of the friendship with your ex-partner.
7. At least in the beginning, limit the amount of information you share with your ex-partner-turned-friend about your current relationship, unless you get permission from the current partner.

Following Joan's advice might be the ideal approach to the new partner issue:

*One of the best ways to make it work is to pick a new partner who is mature enough to handle the fact of your friendship.*

Actually, "mature enough" could probably be more accurately read as *has enough self-esteem*. With this in mind, you can make your friendship more palatable to your current partner by doing what you can to increase his or her self-esteem. By this I do not mean to pump up his or her prideful ego, but rather to support self-esteem through the methods discussed in chapter five. The recent report by the California Task Force to Promote Self-esteem and Personal and Social Responsibility, "Toward a State of Self-Esteem," beautifully suggests ways in which we can build self-esteem in others by:

1. affirming his or her unique worth
2. giving personal attention
3. demonstrating respect, acceptance, and support
4. setting realistic expectations
5. providing a sensible structure for the relationship

6. forgiving him or her
7. supporting him or her in taking risks necessary for growth and self-realization
8. accepting his or her emotional expressions
9. negotiating, rather than being abusive

## Be Supportively Honest

If ex-partners have withdrawn from each other during their recovery from the breakup they will clearly suffer, particularly during the early phase of the breakup when high emotion, confusion, and suspicion often dominate. Without honest communication each partner is forced to try to read the mind of the other. In the gap between them lies fertile ground for misunderstanding and pain which will ultimately make the return to friendship more difficult.

To avoid such misunderstandings and to make the relationship more safe, several people that I interviewed felt that it was helpful when their ex-partners were "supportively honest." *Supportively honest* means that they took the risk of sharing what they were really feeling without resorting to blaming the other for their feelings. It also means that they shared personal information with their ex-partner that helped them understand each other, but didn't share information that was unnecessarily distressing. For example, once you decide to leave the relationship, it is not only important that you communicate why you want to leave but how you feel about the loss of the relationship. On the other hand, while you may feel that your ex-partner became a completely uncaring monster who made you unhappy, it would not be supportively honest or productive to tell him or her that in those terms—be constructive!

In the 1960s and '70s we heard much about the importance of being honest in relationships with others, including family and friends. While most therapists still see honesty as the best policy, awareness has increased both that honest expression of our feelings must be tempered with caring, and that honesty motivated by anger and resentment can be more destructive than useful.

## Avoid Excessive Positive Statements and Associations in the Beginning Phases of Transition to Friendship

The initiator of a breakup, who has had more time to cope with the feelings of separation and loss, etc., may find it easier and less complicated to acknowledge the positive good in their ex-partner sooner than the person who is being left. The "dumpee" may still need the negative thoughts about the initiator in order to hold his or her head up and move on. If your partner is still very upset and dependent upon the relationship (whether initiator or not) it might be advisable for you to at least temporarily avoid excessively positive sentiments. This will be helpful to your partner because it will allow him or her to believe that the relationship is changed, and won't encourage inappropriate hope that the relationship will continue.

If, on the other hand, both partners are well along in their transition prior to the break, each is more free to take care of the other, appreciate the other, mourn the loss of the other. "They may literally and figuratively help each other out the door."[4]

As the marriage unravels, the partners assume and indeed often may self-protectively desire to no longer please each other. And yet among the participants in the study and the many couples I have worked with in therapy, there always appears to be some remnant left of wanting to please the other. The difficult task here is not to erase those feelings but to acknowledge their existence. At the same time, however, you must be aware that their meaning must be redefined in the context of the uncoupled bond. Several of the participants indicated that they had in fact accomplished this change in meaning. Molly, for example, said,

*When I did things for him before it had a different feeling. Now when I do something that I know will please him it doesn't have the same meaning. It doesn't mean that I want us to be together. It means I want him to be happy.*

In Molly's statement is perhaps one of the most common differences between actions performed to please in a coupled relationship and those done after the breakup. Partners in a couple relationship do for each other to some extent to reaffirm the *coupleness* or the boundary around themselves as a unit. The message is, "I do this for you, for us." In couples therapy, my clients often complain that they don't know the "real" motives behind their ex-partner's benevolent acts, and this leaves them feeling confused and uncomfortable.

As Molly and others have shown, it is not necessary to give up or to stop acting upon the desire to please the other. However, after the breakup it is imperative that ex-partners be clear with themselves and with their new partners that the meaning of their action is *not* to regain their sense of being a couple beyond the limits of the friendship they have worked out.

# Postscript

I started this enterprise with the goal of learning about useful strategies for making the often difficult transition from lovers to romantically uncoupled friends and of offering positive messages about the possibilities. I have gained personally from what I have learned about the sometimes courageous, sometimes lighthearted efforts people have made in the interest of maintaining meaningful friendships after the breakup. That so many people have successfully made the transition to enduring friendship, the wide array of personal benefits they accrued for their efforts, and that there are truly concrete things that you can do for yourself and for each other that increase the chances for continued friendship are extremely gratifying and encouraging to me. I hope they are to you as well. Despite the difficulties you may face in the transition and the many confusing, often negative messages you might get from those around you, the opportunity to transform your once-coupled romantic relationship into an uncoupled but very rewarding, enduring friendship is just a choice away.

# Bibliography

This bibliography can't include all of what is available on topics related to breakups and transitions. Instead, these are works that I have found useful for myself and for my clients over the years. Some of them deal with the individual experience of breakup and offer helpful suggestions. Others focus on specific topics such as building self-esteem, focusing emotion, and coping with loss.

Ahrons, Constance R., and Rogers, Roy H. *Divorced Families: Meeting the Challenge of Divorce and Remarriage.* New York: Milton Publishers, 1989.

This extraordinary book approaches divorce as one path of normal adult development rather than as a pathological, primarily negative event. The authors describe the struggles and triumphs that families experience trying to retain some sense of family while they acknowledge the divorce experience. Ahrons and Rogers describe five types of divorced spouses: "perfect pals," "cooperative colleagues," "angry associates," "fiery foes," and "dissolved duos." Perhaps most valuable is the sociological description of families, not just individuals undergoing the divorce experience, and the hope implicit in the fact that many families find successful ways to accomplish the transition to the benefit of all concerned.

Branden, Nathaniel. *How to Raise Your Self Esteem.* New York: Bantam Books, 1988.

Few therapists or authors have given as much of their life energy, time, and commitment to the concept of self-esteem as has Nathaniel Branden. This book balances messages for improving your own self-esteem with the importance of appreciating and accepting others. Its considerable attention to the relationship between social responsibility and personal self-esteem is particularly important in understanding the transition process, because in attempting to understand and support ex-partners, particularly when they're not at their best, we often experience much mental and emotional stress. As Dr. Branden points out, however, in the long run attempts to resolve and be supportive of others in conflict situations can meaningfully support the evolving relationship as well.

Bridges, Williams. *Transitions: Making Sense of Life's Changes.* New York: Wesley, 1980.

This book remains perhaps the best discussion of transitions written today. It focuses on transition experiences in general, however, not specifically on breakups. Among the several important and helpful sections of this book is the presentation of change as a fundamental part of the human experience. Bridges explains that the way in which we cope with change is vital to the way we preserve our emotional, psychological, and spiritual health.

California Task Force to Promote Self-esteem and Personal and Social Responsibility. *Toward a State of Self-esteem.* Sacramento: California State Board of Education, 1990. (Copies of this book may be obtained from the Bureau of Publications, California State Department of Education, P.O. Box 271, Sacramento, CA 95802-0271. The fee for the book is $4 plus 6.5% tax for California residents.

A significant portion of this book is devoted to larger policy issues addressed by state and local officials for building self-esteem in the people of the state. The third and fourth sections define self-esteem and describe key principles for use either by others or by ourselves as individuals in order to nurture self-esteem and our personal and social responsibility. I recommend this book because it is not only important to support your own self-esteem, but also suggests ways of supporting your partner during the transition from lovers to friends.

Colgrov, Nova; Bloomfield, Harold H.; and McWilliams, Peter. *How to Survive the Loss of a Love.* New York: Bantam Books, 1987.

Described by the authors as a "different kind of guide to overcoming all your emotional hurts," this book is beautifully organized. It balances useful suggestions for action with poetic descriptions of experience. This combination enables you to integrate your emotional experience with specific strategies for change, which will lead you toward overcoming the emotional strife of loss. Unfortunately, the authors stress the futility of attempts to reconcile and rekindle the old relationship, and fail to consider how a transition toward a new relationship could happen simultaneously with relinquishing an old relationship.

Crowther, C. Edward, and Stone, Gayle. *Intimacy: Strategies for Successful Relationships.* New York: Dell, 1988.

A good overview of the issue of intimacy, defining the role that it plays in our lives. It offers much information about possible threats to intimacy, and about ways to manage and understand your intimate relationships, as well as how to avoid what the authors describe as "intimacy burnout." I do not know the empirical validity of the workbook and self-tests on intimacy included in the book.

Felder, Leonard. *A Fresh Start: How to Let Go of Emotional Baggage and Enjoy Your Life Again.* New York: Signet Books, 1989.

As the title suggests, *A Fresh Start* focuses on releasing yourself from emotional glitches in life. The author discusses getting out of an emotional rut, letting go of the past, and finding what gets in between what you want in a relationship and what you have.

Fisher, Bruce. *Rebuilding: When Your Relationship Ends.* San Luis Obispo, California: Impact Publishers, 1987.

This is one of the best organized presentations of how to take care of yourself in the divorce/breakup experience. It suggests building blocks of understanding past experiences and working positively for the new. The chapter on letting go is helpful for learning to let go of both the negative and positive feelings associated with your couple relationship. It is unfortunate that Dr. Fisher does not distinguish between impulses to reunite with your ex-partner and impulses to return to the partner under the blanket of denial that the couple relationship is over.

Gendlin, Eugene T. *Focusing.* New York: Bantam Books, 1988.

This is an extraordinary book. Based on years of research, Dr. Gendlin has developed a method of focusing that teaches you to identify and change the way your personal problems concretely exist in your body. With his method you might unlock the physical, felt experience of pain. It is a very useful and direct pathway to releasing yourself for growth.

Halpern, Howard N. *How to Break Your Addiction to a Person.* New York: Bantam Books, 1983.

▼

Dr. Halpern assists you in deciding when to call it quits in the first place. His distinction between being in love and addicted to a person can very quickly help you to sort out the rise of feelings that often plague ex-partners in the breakup process.

Kingma, Daphne Rose. *Coming Apart: Why Relationships End and How to Live Through the Ending of Yours.* New York: Ballantine Books, 1989.

This very easy-to-read book describes why couples break up and why that process is so often difficult. Kingma suggests that breakup can be related to developmental processes experienced by individuals in a relationship. The chapter on the emotional process of parting is concise and helpful. The unconscious processes during parting, which can often go overlooked, can, she suggests, be tapped through understanding dreams or out of the blue thoughts. Understanding these can help you integrate the breakup experience, make it easier to go through, and help you understand its meaning in your life.

A particularly exciting part of this book is its discussion of rituals for parting. It includes techniques for parting in a way that leaves your future brighter and less burdened.

Krantzler, Mel. *Creative Divorce: A New Opportunity for Personal Growth.* New York: Signet Books, 1975.

This ground-breaking work was one of the first to focus on the growth potential inherent in breakups. Written in a very personal style, it lays out an emotional map that can be helpful to you as you go through the process. Of particular value is Mr. Krantzler's approach to coping with the new realities that you will face along the way: from changes in your living circumstances, to other people's responses, to new relationships, and to a new you.

McKay, Matthew; Davis, Marth; and Fanning, Patrick. *Messages: The Communication Book.* Oakland, CA: New Harbinger Publications, 1983.

As familiar as the notion that poor communication is the root of all evil in relationships has become, it *is* essential. This book is the best, most comprehensive work that I have seen on the subject.

McKay, Matthew, and Fanning, Patrick. *Self-Esteem.* New York: St. Martin's Press, 1988.

Unique to this book is the important concept of the "pathological critic," or the tendency to be excessively and destructively self-critical. This "pathological critic" reveals itself when we use inappropriate "shoulds" in our internal conversation with ourselves.

Schellenbaum, Peter. *How to Say No to the One You Love.* Wilmette, IL: Chiron Publications, 1987.

A Swiss Jungian analyst discusses the delicate but important balances in intimate relationships. This balance of the needs of the individual to remain separate and the needs of the couple to join is only now becoming understood. A bit difficult reading in some places but worth the effort.

Trafford, Abigail. *Crazy Time: Surviving Divorce.* New York: Bantam Books, 1984.

A detailed description of the divorce experience, *Crazy Time* handles, in some detail, its crazy-making, out-of-proportion, and surprising aspects. In a section less developed than that on divorce, Ms. Trafford explores the recovery process, offering some suggestions for a successful recovery from the emotional ravages of breakup. Of particular value here is the first chapter of the recovery section, on the emergence of a self. The section on the impact of the divorce experience and our way of understanding love with respect to reality and fantasy may be very helpful, since often relationships break up because of misunderstanding about love and about how one can both love and be loved in the context of a romantic relationship.

van der Hart, Onno, ed. *Coping with Loss: The Therapeutic Use of Leave-Taking Rituals.* New York: Irvington Publishers, 1988.

This collection of articles defines leave-taking rituals as a way of assisting people to cope with the loss of a loved one, a loss of some important aspect of themselves, or of a life experience. Though written for therapists, a lay audience can gather much from it. Dr. van der Hart succinctly describes its intent: "This book is about people who have had traumatic experiences or who have suffered severe losses, the memories of which continue to haunt them, and it is about a therapeutic approach which has been designed to help them. What this involves, in essence, is that by leave-taking of the key symbols that keep alive the traumatic memories of the person who is no longer there, the client takes leave of the actual memories or the actual person." (p. 7)

Vaughn, Diane. *Uncoupling: Turning Points in Intimate Relationships.* New York: Oxford University Press, 1986.

Although this comprehensive, scholarly description of the uncoupling of intimate relationships is so thorough as to make for laborious reading it is worth the effort. It describes in detail

▼

processes readily visible to all of us related to the uncoupling experience, and at the same time, reveals many of the covert, hidden aspects that couples collaboratively attempt to conceal and which you may not have noticed. If you are the one who has initiated the breakup in your relationship, the chapter on partners in transition can be very helpful in building your compassion and understanding for your partner's experiences. If you are at the state of beginning to think about breaking up, some of what Dr. Vaughn discusses may be helpful in either assisting you in your decision to break up, or understanding paths for transforming your current relationship as an alternative to breaking up.

Welwood, John, ed. *Challenge of the Heart: Love, Sex and Intimacy in Changing Times.* Boston, MA: Shambahala, 1985.

This is a super collection of readings on love, sex, and intimacy. It can open your eyes to many views of love—take what you like, leave what you don't.

# Endnotes

## Introduction

1. Miss Manners, *San Francisco Chronicle* (April 27, 1990).
2. Survey reported in K. Kressel, M. Lopez-Morillas, J. Weinglass, and M. Deutsch, "Professional Intervention in Divorce: A Summary of the Views of Lawyers, Psychotherapists and Clergy," *Journal of Divorce* (2), 1978, 119–55.
3. Carol J. Masheter, "Postdivorce Relationships Between Exspouses," Doctoral Dissertation, University of Connecticut, 1988. Constance R. Ahrons and Roy H. Rodgers, *Divorced Families: Meeting the Challenge of Divorce and Remarriage* (New York: Milton Publishers, 1989), p. 45.

## Chapter 1

1. From a column written by Liz Smith, *San Francisco Chronicle* (May, 1990).

## Chapter 2

1. C. Cluckhohn, H. Murray, and D. Schneider, *Personality in Nature, Society, and Culture* (New York: Knopf, 1953) p. 53.
2. Ahrons and Rodgers in their book *Divorced Families* describe five types of postdivorce relationships: perfect pals, cooperative colleagues, angry associates, fiery foes, and dissolved duos. Most of the couples I interviewed were perfect pals or at least cooperative colleagues at the time I interviewed them. In their transition from lovers to friends couples can and do relate in ways that can be described as angry associates and fiery foes. But for many reasons some ultimately change to become more friendly. This change over time is, of course important for the hope it might engender in those who desire to move forward in their currently negative postbreakup relationships. Exemplifying an awareness of this change, June, a 32-year-old mother and ballet dancer whom I interviewed, said:

*Since it's only been a month since he decided that he was not available for a committed relationship, it's really hard to know just what we are to each other. So, each time we connect, a lot of feeling comes up. One of the feelings is a sense of friendship. We don't see much of each other for now because it's just too painful and difficult. But with the help I'm getting I am sure that when I am able to let go, his friendship will mean the world to me.*

## Chapter 3

1. John Welwood, *Challenge of the Heart*. (Boston: Shambhala Publications, Inc., 1985).

2. John J. Macionis, "Intimacy: Structure and Process in Interpersonal Relationships," *Alternative Life Styles* (1978) pp. 113–130.

3. Macionis, "Intimacy."

4. Isolina Ricci, *Mom's House, Dad's House: Making Shared Custody Work* (New York: Macmillan Publishing Company, 1980) p. 89.

5. Keith E. Davis, "Near and Dear: Friendship and Love Compared," *Psychology Today* 19 (1985) pp. 22–30.

## Chapter 4

1. Thanks to the staff members of the Contra Costa Battered Women's Alternative for many of the items on this list.

2. Judith S. Wallerstein and Joan Berlin Kelly, *Surviving the Breakup* (New York: Basic Books, 1988) p. 75.

## Chapter 5

1. Williams Bridges, *Transitions: Making Sense of Life's Changes* (New York: Wesley, 1980); Nancy K. Schlossberg, *Counseling*

*Adults in Transition* (New York: Springer Publishing Company, 1984).

2. California Task Force to Promote Self-esteem and Personal and Social Responsibility, *Toward a State of Self-esteem* (Sacramento: California State Department of Education Bureau of Publications, 1990).

3. Special thanks to Jeri Marlowe, M.A., for suggesting this technique.

4. The notion of reframing as a change-inducing tactic was developed some years ago by a group of interactional therapists, otherwise known as the Palo Alto Group, at the MRI in Palo Alto, California.

5. Special thanks to Will MacDonald who gave this technique to Dr. Francine Shapiro, who in turn gave it to me.

6. Diane Vaughn, *Uncoupling: Turning Points in Intimate Relationships* (New York: Oxford University Press, 1986) p. 177.

7. Masheter, "Postdivorce Relationships Between Exspouses," p. 129.

8. Nicky Hart, *When Marriage Ends: A Study in Status Passage* (London: Tavistock, 1976); cited in Vaughn, *Uncoupling*, pp. 116–17.

9. Isolina Ricci, *Mom's House, Dad's House*, p. 89.

10. Special thanks to Lonnie Barbach, Ph.D., for this exercise.

11. Weiss, R. S., *Marital Separation* (New York: Basic Books, 1975).

**Chapter 6**

1. Peter Schellenbaum, *How to Say No to the One You Love* (Wilmette, IL: Chiron Publications, 1987).

2. Vaughn, *Uncoupling*, p. 174.

3. Bruce Fisher, *Rebuilding When Your Relationship Ends* (San Luis Obispo, CA: Impact Publishers, 1987). "Dumpee" is Bruce Fisher's term for the member of a couple who did not initiate the breakup.

4. Vaughn, *Uncoupling*, p. 174.

# Index

# Notes

# Notes